Freedom of Religion and Belief in Turkey

"This is a timely book on the freedom of religion and belief in Turkey at a seminal point in its modern history. Using both international and domestic law, the book examines important issues relating to private beliefs, minority rights and their standing, as well as state involvement in religion and the impact on Turkey's secularity."
—Leonard Hammer, Professor, *University of Arizona*

"Focusing specifically on five drastic issues, to be compelled to reveal one's religion and beliefs; conscientious objection; compulsory religious education; recognition of faith groups; religious symbols and dress, all in the framework of religion/belief, society and politics in Turkey, is a very timely and valuable contribution to the field."
—Dr İştar Gözaydın, Professor of Law & Politics—2017 *University of Oslo, Lisl and Leo Eitinger Human Rights Award winner*

"In July 2020 President Erdoğan decreed that the Hagia Sophia in İstanbul, built as an Orthodox Christian church, should once again become a mosque. Özgür H. Çınar has written the definitive, lucid, and readable, guide to understanding the issues at stake in Erdoğan's decisive break with 86 years of secularism in Turkey. This new book is highly recommended."
—Bill Bowring, Professor of Law, *Birkbeck College, University of London, UK*

"This volume will prove to be one of the most important contributions to the field of human rights, in general, and to freedom of religion and belief, in particular. Libraries and scholars should have it as a reference, as should judges, lawyers, and public administrators. University and college courses in public policy, philosophy, religion, or in comparative and international law will find it very useful."
—Winston Langley, Professor Emeritus, *University of Massachusetts, Boston*

Özgür Heval Çınar

Freedom of Religion and Belief in Turkey

Religion, Society and Politics

Özgür Heval Çınar
School of Law and Criminology
University of Greenwich
London, UK

ISBN 978-3-030-70076-8   ISBN 978-3-030-70077-5 (eBook)
https://doi.org/10.1007/978-3-030-70077-5

© The Author(s), under exclusive license to Springer Nature Switzerland AG 2021
This work is subject to copyright. All rights are solely and exclusively licensed by the Publisher, whether the whole or part of the material is concerned, specifically the rights of translation, reprinting, reuse of illustrations, recitation, broadcasting, reproduction on microfilms or in any other physical way, and transmission or information storage and retrieval, electronic adaptation, computer software, or by similar or dissimilar methodology now known or hereafter developed.
The use of general descriptive names, registered names, trademarks, service marks, etc. in this publication does not imply, even in the absence of a specific statement, that such names are exempt from the relevant protective laws and regulations and therefore free for general use.
The publisher, the authors and the editors are safe to assume that the advice and information in this book are believed to be true and accurate at the date of publication. Neither the publisher nor the authors or the editors give a warranty, expressed or implied, with respect to the material contained herein or for any errors or omissions that may have been made. The publisher remains neutral with regard to jurisdictional claims in published maps and institutional affiliations.

Cover pattern © Melisa Hasan

This Palgrave Macmillan imprint is published by the registered company Springer Nature Switzerland AG.
The registered company address is: Gewerbestrasse 11, 6330 Cham, Switzerland

Contents

1 Introduction   1

2 The Religion Box on the National Identity Card: Being Compelled to Reveal One's Religion and Beliefs   7

3 The Military-Nation and Conscientious Objectors   35

4 Unresolved Issue: Compulsory Religious Education   57

5 Recognition of Faith Groups and the Opening of Places of Worship   81

6 The Manifestation of Religious Belief in the Public Sphere: Religious Symbols and Dress   115

Index   141

About the Author

Özgür Heval Çınar is a lawyer. Presently, he is an associate professor at the University of Greenwich, School of Law and Criminology. He completed his PhD at the School of Law, University of Essex. Previously, he was a post-doc fellow at the University of Oxford between 2012 and 2016.

CHAPTER 1

Introduction

Abstract All the chapters in this book focus on issues that are test cases pertaining to the question as to whether the right to freedom of religion or belief receives adequate protection and whether real equality has been attained in Turkey. In other words, they illustrate the current state of the freedom of religion or belief in Turkey and the challenges and complex problems facing it, and they contribute to the understanding of Turkish secularism and religious freedom and the problems suffered by believers and non-believers in the society. The chapters also enrich debate on the process of democratisation in Turkey.

Keywords Freedom of thought, conscience and religion • Society • Politics • Turkey • International and domestic/national law • *Forum internum and externum*

The freedom of thought, conscience and religion, from which stem the tenets of pluralism, tolerance and open-mindedness, is one of the most basic freedoms of a democratic society. For those who believe in God it is a key facet of their identity and their conception of life, but it is also important for people who possess no beliefs, such as atheists, agnostics and sceptics.

There are several international human rights documents that safeguard the freedom of thought, conscience and religion (e.g. article 18 of both the Universal Declaration of Human Rights and International Covenant on Civil and Political Rights, article 9 of the European Convention on Human Rights—ECHR). The Republic of Turkey (hereafter 'Turkey') is a signatory to these conventions, but in practice it has rarely lived up to its obligations.

The Justice and Development Party (*Adalet ve Kalkınma Partisi— AKP*) came to power in Turkey, a country seeking to join the European Union (EU), in 2002. The AKP has pledged to introduce freedoms and has made some significant legal changes in line with the political criteria of the EU. However, it has failed to address many restrictions related to the freedom of thought, conscience and religion.

Turkey was named in the 2019 report of the United States Commission on International Religious Freedom as one of the countries where the most serious contraventions of religious freedoms take place, identifying state interference in the *forum internum* as the most flagrant of these violations. Other international governmental and non-governmental organisations, such as the United Nations Special Rapporteur on Freedom of Religion or Belief and EU Progress Reports, mention the same problems.[1]

In this book efforts will be made to understand the situation as regards the right to freedom of religion and belief in Turkey, concentrating on the most topical issues. In its constitution Turkey is proclaimed to be a democratic and secular state. While religion has always been an important part of Turkey's social and political life, it is only in more recent times that issues concerning religious freedom have been raised in the sphere of human rights. Demands for remedies of human rights violations have challenged the traditional relationship between State and religion. The recent process of drawing up a new constitution has seen fierce debate over the thorny issue of how freedom of religion or belief should be safeguarded and demands that the State maintain an equal distance to all religions or beliefs in the country to aid pluralism and equality have challenged the status quo.

All the chapters in this book focus on issues that are test cases pertaining to the question as to whether the right to freedom of religion or belief receives adequate protection and whether real equality has been attained in Turkey. In other words, they illustrate the current state of the freedom of religion or belief in Turkey and the challenges and complex problems facing it, and they contribute to the understanding of Turkish secularism and religious freedom and the problems suffered by believers and non-believers in the society. The chapters also enrich debate on the process of democratisation in Turkey.

Before summarising below what each chapter of the book explains, it should be noted that each chapter has been written with the same structure. Firstly, answers are sought as to what provisions exist in international law with regard to the subject in question. In the chapter on international law in particular the judgments of the European Court of Human Rights (ECtHR) are closely examined. This is followed by looking at the historical origins of the issue and a study of the relevant provisions in Turkish law and the attitude of Turkish courts with reference to key judgments. After this examination the parallels and conflicting interpretations between Turkish law and international law are revealed and a road map regarding what Turkey must do is set out.

Chapter 2 looks at Turkish secularism with reference to the religion box on Turkish identity cards. By initially setting out international norms, it explains in detail the process by which the ECtHR made its judgment recognising an individual's right not to be obliged to disclose his/her beliefs. It also undertakes a critical examination of the approach of local courts and of the Constitutional Court and emphasises the cooperation which exists between the religious authority, the Directorate of Religious Affairs (*Diyanet İşleri Başkanlığı-Diyanet*) and the secular courts. Although the Turkish Constitution is clear that an individual is not obliged to declare his/her religion or beliefs, the presence of a religion box on identity cards is considered lawful. This contradiction exists on account of the fact that the Turkish type of secularism, a cornerstone of the system in Turkey, permits such anomalies.

Chapter 3 examines another controversial issue that is central to the freedom of religion or belief: the right to conscientious objection to military service. While providing an analysis based on human rights, it also explores the historical background to this right in Turkey and includes sociological analysis. Turkey has not met its international human rights obligations in this field, whereby it is bound to protect the right to conscientious objection. It has not enacted legislation recognising this fundamental right, resulting in the ECtHR repeatedly finding that Turkey has violated article 9 of the ECHR. Turkey's refusal to introduce legislation is also examined.

Chapter 4 also looks at compulsory religious education in Turkey. The issue of religious education has been the subject of debate in Turkey ever since the founding of the Republic in 1923 on account of its perceived

Sunni Islam slant. Since Turkey began the process of joining the EU this debate has intensified. The *Hasan and Eylem Zengin* and *Mansur Yalçın and others* judgments[2] at the ECtHR have led to closer attention being paid to Turkey's obligations regarding international law. It questions whether this 'religious education' is exclusively of Sunni Islamic beliefs and whether there should be compulsory religious education in schools. The history of religious instruction in Turkey and the current legal situation are also explored.

Chapter 5 addresses the question of places of worship. This includes the right for a religion or belief to have a legal personality, the right to open a place of worship, the right to teach one's religion and belief, and the right of a religion to appoint its own religious officials. In this chapter the point is made that despite some legislative changes in the EU harmonisation process, the right to establish places of worship has yet to receive adequate protection. This is true for more recent religious communities like the Protestants and Jehovah's Witnesses, in addition to the Alevi community that the largest religious/faith minority community in Turkey, which makes it hard to ignore.[3] The Alevis have for years complained that the State has persecuted them by imposing a Sunni understanding of Islam. As regards the Alevis, the main issue seems to be whether the authorities consider their *cem* (gathering) houses to be legitimate places of worship. Despite the Treaty of Lausanne protecting the rights of non-Muslims, they also face problems. In this chapter, there is a discussion of the administrative obstacles that make it very difficult for Protestant churches and kingdom halls of the Jehovah's Witnesses to gain place of worship status. It also criticises the ECtHR's approach in cases relating to places of worship and argues that international compliance control mechanisms should apply stricter scrutiny in such cases.

Chapter 6 looks at religious symbols and dress (garments) such as the headscarf, a subject of debate in Europe. The ban on wearing the headscarf—which was only recently lifted—preventing women working as public servants covering the head, is examined in connection to the transition from the Ottoman Empire to the Republic. Following the elections of 2011, which the AKP won with nearly 50% of the vote, reforms were introduced that implemented its main policies and practices. This chapter explores whether these reforms prove that the AKP has Islamic fundamentalist policies and argues that as the most sensitive issue has been resolved, the problems faced by religious minorities should be addressed.

In conclusion, there is no doubt that Turkey must introduce legislative changes that establish a legal framework that provides adequate safeguards for the right to freedom of religion or belief for all. If no changes are forthcoming, or if the situation gets worse, people will not have the right to manifest their identity or to freely exercise their civil and political rights and freedoms. During Turkey's accession process to the EU, there has been, quite properly, scrutiny of Turkey's approach to this fundamental right.

It is my hope that this book will assist those wishing to understand this question. I wish to offer my warmest personal thanks to Palgrave Macmillan, Ms Hülya Ak, Mr Andrew Penny and all those others who have offered valuable assistance and encouragement but are not mentioned here.

Notes

1. See, for example, United Nations Special Rapporteur on Freedom of Religion or Belief, 'Interim report of the Special Rapporteur of the Commission on Human Rights on the elimination of all forms of intolerance and of discrimination based on religion or belief: Situation in Turkey', 11 August 2000, A/55/280/Add.1; European Commission, '2013 Regular Report on Turkey's Progress Towards Accession', 16 October 2013, SWD(2013)417 Final; European Commission, '2012 Regular Report on Turkey's Progress Towards Accession', 10 October 2012, SWD(2012)336 Final.
2. *Hasan and Eylem Zengin v. Turkey*, 9 October 2007, No. 1448/04; *Mansur Yalçın and others v. Turkey*, 26 September 2014, No. 21163/11.
3. International Religious Freedom Reports, (2019), 'Turkey: USCIRF–Recommended for Special Watch List', p. 82, https://www.uscirf.gov/sites/default/files/Turkey.pdf, accessed 21 September 2020.

CHAPTER 2

The Religion Box on the National Identity Card: Being Compelled to Reveal One's Religion and Beliefs

Abstract This chapter addresses international norms by exploring the European Court of Human Rights' case law in particular regarding an individual's right not to be obliged to disclose his/her beliefs. It also examines the approach of local courts (especially the Constitutional Court) in Turkey. At this juncture this chapter asks certain questions such as if Turkey is a secular state, why does it need to know the religion of its citizens. Does Turkey comply with international law?

Keywords Religion and belief • National identity card • Turkey • International and domestic/national law • *Forum internum*

2.1 INTRODUCTION

The system of birth certificates/identity cards in Turkey dates back to the year 1881 during the Ottoman era. Amongst European Union (EU) member states and candidate member states Turkey is the only one to record the religion of its citizens. Hence, following a change in the law in 2016, new identity cards feature a chip containing various information. Data pertaining to an individual's beliefs is not visible on the identity card. However, this information is still recorded on the system within the framework of Personal Data Protection, and public institutions are able to see the information on the chip on their systems. But what is not clear is which public bodies can see this data. In this context, this amendment

© The Author(s), under exclusive license to Springer Nature Switzerland AG 2021
Ö. H. Çınar, *Freedom of Religion and Belief in Turkey*,
https://doi.org/10.1007/978-3-030-70077-5_2

brought in after the European Court of Human Rights (ECtHR) judgment in the *Sinan Işık* case in 2010 has still not removed the risk that citizens might suffer discrimination. In fact, in the event of citizens not answering the question on the chip regarding religious belief, there is an increased risk of discrimination in that a person will face questions from public bodies regarding why they did not write Islam. Consequently, in Turkey, when determining a citizen's identity, Turkishness and Islam are defined as two important elements. In line with this political and sociological reality it is worth undertaking a discussion of the fact that although this information is not visible on an identity card, the authorities can access it and people are still pressured to reveal their beliefs.

At this juncture there are certain questions that need to be asked. The first of these is related to the questions as to whether Turkey is really secular and whether freedom of belief exists there. Secondly, if Turkey is a secular state, why does it need to know the religion of its citizens? Thirdly, international law places emphasis on the *forum internum* dimension of the freedom of religion and belief, stating that people shall never under any circumstances be coerced into revealing their beliefs. On this point does this application in Turkey comply with international law? Might it lead to discrimination between citizens? In particular, a close examination of the ECtHR judgment in the *Sinan Işık* case will be undertaken and its effects on Turkey probed.

2.2 INTERNATIONAL LAW STANDARDS

Freedom of thought, conscience and religion are recognised in all general international and regional human rights texts.[1] In modern human rights law, the first document to protect the freedom of thought, conscience and religion was the Universal Declaration of Human Rights (UDHR), which was drawn up in 1948. Article 18 of this document is of great significance as it defined the parameters of freedom of thought, conscience and religion for all subsequent international norms, in particular the International Covenant on Civil and Political Rights (ICCPR) and the European Convention on Human Rights (ECHR). Article 18 of the UDHR states:

> Everyone has the right to freedom of thought, conscience and religion; this right includes freedom to change his religion or belief, and freedom, either alone or in community with others and in public or private, to manifest his religion or belief in teaching, practice, worship and observance.

Article 18 is made up of two parts. The first of these guarantees everyone's right to freedom of thought, conscience and religion, the freedoms of 'thought' and 'conscience' being closely connected to freedom of 'religion' in this part.[2] The second part of this article is divided into two sections defining the right to freedom of thought, conscience and religion. In the first section is the term "freedom to change his religion or belief", while in the second "freedom, either alone or in community with others and in public or private, to manifest his religion or belief in teaching, practice, worship and observance". The first part of this definition relates to the internal sphere, the *forum internum*, of this right, and the second relates to the *forum externum*, the external sphere of it.[3] Concerning the *forum internum*, this relates to the private realm of the individual, who is completely free to determine his/her destiny.[4]

Boyle and Partsch stress that the UDHR's recognition of the human being and the moral autonomy of the individual as formulated in article 18 is its essence.[5] Article 1 of the same document supports this interpretation, saying that "[a]ll human beings are born free and equal in dignity and rights. They are endowed with reason and conscience and should act towards one another in a spirit of brotherhood." The main emphasis of the UDHR recognises as absolute and subject to no limitation the internal sphere of freedom of thought, conscience and religion. The state, therefore, has no right to intervene in the *forum internum* aspect of freedom of thought, conscience and religion.[6] However, as for the *forum externum* of this freedom, this is subject to some limitations. Some general limitations regarding human rights and freedoms were included in articles 29 and 30 by the UDHR's drafters.

When article 18 is read along with article 2 of the same document, it should be pointed out that the freedom of thought, conscience and religion cannot be subjected to discrimination. Although in countries, such as Turkey, that have signed the UDHR, it is not legally binding, but it is still recognised as an important political and ethical document.

The second important document drafted by the United Nations is the ICCPR of 1966. Article 18 of this document safeguards the freedom of thought, conscience and religion in the following way:

1. Everyone shall have the right to freedom of thought, conscience and religion. This right shall include freedom to have or to adopt a religion or belief of his choice, and freedom, either individually or in community with others and in public or private, to manifest his religion or belief in worship, observance, practice and teaching.

2. No one shall be subject to coercion which would impair his freedom to have or to adopt a religion or belief of his choice.
3. Freedom to manifest one's religion or beliefs may be subject only to such limitations as are prescribed by law and are necessary to protect public safety, order, health or morals or the fundamental rights and freedoms of others.
4. The States Parties to the present Covenant undertake to have respect for the liberty of parents and, when applicable, legal guardians to ensure the religious and moral education of their children in conformity with their own convictions.

The four paragraphs of this article emphasise similar concepts to those contained in article 18 of the UDHR (see para.1).[7] Article 4(2) of the ICCPR states that "[n]o derogation from articles 6, 7, 8 (paragraphs 1 and 2), 11, 15, 16 and 18 may be made under this provision". Hence, Boyle makes clear that under the protection of this international instrument the individual has an absolute right to freedom of thought, conscience and religion.[8] However, one should remember that although article 18 guarantees freedom of thought, conscience and religion in the public sphere in addition to the private sphere, the freedom to manifest one's religion or belief, that is, the *forum externum* of freedom, is not absolute and may be subject to limitations.[9]

The Human Rights Committee (HRC) has made efforts to broaden the scope of guaranteed freedoms with its observations. In 1993 in its 22nd General Comment it addressed the question of the obligations states have as regards the freedom of thought, conscience and religion.[10] It emphasised that both religious beliefs without a god and non-belief were within the scope of the freedom of belief. And also, HRC stated: "The Committee therefore views with concern any tendency to discriminate against any religion or belief for any reason, including the fact that they are newly established, or represent religious minorities that may be the subject of hostility on the part of a predominant religious community."[11] In addition, this General Comment underlined the *forum internum* as follows:

> Article 18 distinguishes the freedom of thought, conscience, religion or belief from the freedom to manifest religion or belief. It does not permit any limitations whatsoever on the freedom of thought and conscience or on the freedom to have or adopt a religion or belief of one's choice. These freedoms are protected unconditionally, as is the right of everyone to hold opin-

ions without interference in article 19.1. In accordance with articles 18.2 and 17, *no one can be compelled to reveal his thoughts or adherence to a religion or belief.*[12]

The ECHR was drafted in 1950. Article 9 of the Convention safeguards this freedom thus:

1. Everyone has the right to freedom of thought, conscience and religion; this right includes freedom to change his religion or belief and freedom, either alone or in community with others and in public or private, to manifest his religion or belief, in worship, teaching, practice and observance.
2. Freedom to manifest one's religion or beliefs shall be subject only to such limitations as are prescribed by law and are necessary in a democratic society in the interests of public safety, for the protection of public order, health or morals, or for the protection of the rights and freedoms of others.

The first paragraph is identical to article 18 of the UDHR and consists of two parts. The first part, up to the semicolon, guarantees everyone's right to freedom of thought, conscience and religion unconditionally. It is important to remember that article 9 also safeguards freedom of thought and conscience, not just religious beliefs,[13] so it includes atheists, agnostics, sceptics and the unconcerned.[14]

The second part of the first paragraph protects the freedom to manifest one's religion or belief.[15] Of the two paragraphs, the first permits "freedom to change his religion or belief"[16] and the second mentions "freedom, either alone or in community with others and in public or private, to manifest his religion or belief in teaching, practice, worship and observance". As explained in more detail under articles 18 of the UDHR and the ICCPR this makes clear that the former relates to the internal sphere, the *forum internum*, while the latter relates to the external sphere, the *forum externum*.[17]

Murdoch writes, "[P]rotection of personal thought, conscience and belief obviously begins with rights to hold and to change these beliefs, this involves the area often referred to as the *forum internum*."[18] Hence, article 9 mainly protects the private sphere.[19] However, in certain circumstances, the *forum externum* (freedom to manifest one's religion or beliefs) may be restricted by domestic law.[20]

In addition, it should be noted that states must also read article 9 in conjunction with article 14 which states, "The enjoyment of the rights and freedoms set forth in this Convention shall be secured without discrimination on any ground such as sex, race, colour, language, religion, political or other opinion, national or social origin, association with a national minority, property, birth or other status."

One of the key differences between the ICCPR and the ECHR is that under the ECHR's derogation article, article 15, freedom of thought, conscience and religion is not a non-derogable right. Article 15, paragraph 2, cites certain articles (articles 2, 3, 4(1) and 7) as embodying non-derogable rights, but not article 9.[21] However, as it is almost inconceivable to imagine a case that would 'strictly require' interference from the state in a believer's *forum internum*, some scholars boldly claim that the right to freedom of thought, conscience and religion is non-derogable under article 15, even though it is not mentioned in that article.[22] It is noteworthy that the constitutions of some European countries—such as article 15 of the Turkish Constitution—clearly state that the right to religious freedom may not be derogated in time of war and/or public emergency (e.g. the Constitutions of Poland, article 233(1) and Portugal, article 19(6)).

Article 10 of the Charter of Fundamental Rights of the EU accepted in 2000 states:

1. Everyone has the right to freedom of thought, conscience and religion. This right includes freedom to change religion or belief and freedom, either alone or in community with others and in public or in private, to manifest religion or belief, in worship, teaching, practice and observance.
2. The right to conscientious objection is recognised, in accordance with the national laws governing the exercise of this right.

Article 21 of this Charter makes clear that discrimination based on religion or belief is not permissible, and article 22 promises that the EU will respect religious diversity.

To sum up, the freedom of thought, conscience and religion is one of the fundamental freedoms in international human rights law which are defined as non-derogable. There are two dimensions of this freedom—the *forum internum* and the *forum externum*. The *forum internum* dimension focuses on a person being forced to behave in contravention of this freedom. In other words, states are not allowed to intervene in this sphere. In this respect, states cannot force a person to reveal his/her religion or belief in an identity card or in somewhere else. However, the manifestation of religion or belief, which is accepted as *forum externum*, is subject to limitations. Although such restrictions are necessary in a democratic society, the principle of proportionality must be adhered to. International human rights law also stresses that discrimination based on religion or belief is unacceptable.

In international law although these are the general rules it is important to emphasise the judgments of the ECtHR on these issues as it provides the fundamental protection in Europe for human rights. In particular, the issue of states gathering information on citizens' religion concerns the *forum internum* dimension of this freedom, that is, a person's right to not be compelled to reveal their beliefs. A close examination will be made of Court judgments relating to this topic, particularly of the judgment in the *Sinan Işık* case.

2.2.1   European Court of Human Rights' Case Law

The first judgment of the ECtHR regarding the right not to be compelled to reveal one's beliefs was the 2001 *Saniewski v. Poland* judgment.[23] In this case the applicant, who attended a state secondary school in the town of Pionki, received his school report on 20 June 1997 for the academic year 1996/97. In the report was a list of courses which he had attended, including 'religion/ethics', with the marks he had been awarded. The 'religion/ethics' course mark was left blank. Similarly, the place for marks awarded for other subjects such as 'informatics', 'music' and 'fine arts' were also blank. The applicant complained about his school report, claiming his freedom of thought, conscience and religion had been violated as the fact no mark had been awarded in the religion/ethics course indicated that he had not attended this course. He had consequently been compelled to publicly reveal his beliefs. He declared that he was an atheist, which in Poland, a staunchly Catholic country intolerant of such views, meant his chances of going to university or finding a good job were seriously affected.

The Court, 'leaving open the question of whether article 9 of the Convention guarantees a right to remain silent as to one's religious beliefs', stressed that the applicant had not grounded his claim of risk of stigmatisation on concrete events. The Court firstly noted that the applicant's complaint about his school report related only to one school year when he was young, and the applicant admitted he would not be obliged to present it during an application to a university or when looking for a job. Consequently, he had not backed up his claim that the report could adversely affect his educational or employment prospects. Hence, the Court found insufficient evidence that the school report in question would have any effect on the applicant's future. Secondly, the Court also took into account the fact that on the school report there were no marks awarded for other subjects such as 'informatics', 'music' and 'fine arts'. For this reason, it was not possible to understand from the report whether the applicant had refused to attend these courses or whether these courses had not taken place in his school during that school year. Thirdly, the Court observed that religious discrimination in Poland is prohibited by both domestic law and International Labour Organisation Conventions. Consequently, there would be a remedy available to the applicant in case of any effect the school report might have on his finding employment in the future. Fourthly, the Court noted that the applicant had not claimed to have experienced any difficulties on account of the school report in question. He had not mentioned any animosity being shown to him, or other incidents of intolerance. He had also not argued he had been discriminated against because of his atheism, either by a public authority or by any private person or entity. Hence, the Court found that the applicant had not demonstrated that he had experienced adverse consequences from the school report that would constitute an interference with his rights and freedoms safeguarded by article 9 of the Convention.[24]

When the judgment is evaluated in its entirety, the first problematic issue is that possible discriminatory treatment that the applicant might face as an atheist in Catholic-majority Poland was not taken into consideration. The Court burdened the applicant with having to prove that he was a victim of discrimination. Apart from this, the Court took particular care to avoid commenting on the right not to be compelled to reveal one's belief.[25]

The Court subsequently handed down a judgment regarding the box for religion on identity cards in Greece in the *Sofianopoulos and others v. Greece* case in 2002.[26] The fact that in this judgment the Court dealt with an individual's right not to declare their religious beliefs under the *forum internum* dimension is important. The applicants in this case did not demand the removal of the box for religion on identity cards; instead they claimed that the Greek state had violated their right to manifest their beliefs by completely removing it from identity cards. The Court noted the state's view regarding the reason for data being on an identity card, that is, in order to check the card owner's identity, meant that information such as fingerprints, spouse's name and forename, gender, occupation, nationality, home address and religion were not necessary. The Court concluded that an identity card cannot be seen as an instrument for members of any religion or faith to make public their beliefs. It agreed that an identity card is not absolutely necessary for the functioning of society, which is apparent since several states use other official documents such as passports or driving licences to identify citizens. However, the Court concluded that if a State introduces identity cards, they should be seen solely as official documents for the purpose of identifying persons as citizens. The Court agreed with the local authority that a person's religion was not information that should be utilised to determine a citizen's relationship to the State. Such things may change in addition to being a matter of conscience for the individual concerned. Furthermore, to have such information in a document risked exposing the holders to circumstances in their contacts with the authorities that might lead to discrimination. This is also the case in their professional lives. The Court drew attention to the fact that in Greece the Orthodox Church is the dominant religion and that religious ceremonies often take place at official events. This does not warrant recording religion in identity cards, as argued by the applicants. The Court emphasised that the purpose of an identity card was not to reinforce the religious feelings of the holder of the card or to display the religious feelings of society. The Court hence concluded there had been no breach of the applicants' right to manifest their religion.[27]

In this judgment, the Court attached particular importance to the risk of discrimination, unlike in the Saniewski judgment. However, by not addressing the essential issue of a person's right not to be compelled to reveal their religious beliefs, the judgment is deficient.[28] The Court passed down its first judgment relating to an individual's being forced to disclose their religious beliefs constituting by itself a possible violation of the Convention in the case of *Folgerø and others v. Norway* in 2007.[29] In this case the Norwegian Humanist Association had assisted three sets of parents to file a case against the Norwegian Government, claiming that the KRL (*Kristendomskunnskap med religions- og livssynsorientering—Christianity, Religion and Philosophy*) brought into State schools in 1993 was not objective, critical and pluralistic. In this case the Court found there had been a breach of the right to education under article 2 of Protocol No. 1 of the Convention, with one of the grounds cited being the right of an individual not to be compelled to divulge their beliefs. The

Court noted that information relating to personal religious and philosophical beliefs concerned the most intimate aspects of private life. The Court found that despite parents not being obliged to declare their beliefs and the school authorities having been notified of the necessity of observing parents' right to respect for private life, a risk existed that the parents could feel they were in a position where they were compelled to reveal their deeply held religious and philosophical beliefs to the school authorities.[30]

The Court followed this judgment with further judgments along the same lines, in *Alexandridis v. Greece*[31] and *Dimitras and others v. Greece*.[32] In the case of *Alexandridis v. Greece* the applicant was a lawyer who took the oath of office at Athens Court of First Instance on 2 November 2005, it being a precondition of practising as a lawyer. The applicant claimed that when swearing the oath, he had had to divulge the fact that he was not an Orthodox Christian. The Court noted that the freedom to manifest one's beliefs also had a negative aspect, in that the individual had a right not to be compelled to manifest his/her religion or religious beliefs and not to feel coerced into behaving in a manner that would permit others to judge whether he/she had—or did not have—such beliefs. The Court consequently found that as the applicant had been compelled to disclose to the court the fact that he was not a member of the Greek Orthodox Church his freedom not to have to manifest his religious beliefs, safeguarded by article 9, had been violated.[33] In summary, the Court concluded that the State authorities had no jurisdiction as regards intervening in the sphere of an individual's freedom of conscience, enquiring into their religious beliefs or compelling them to reveal their opinions concerning theological matters.[34]

The applicants in the case of *Dimitras and others v. Greece* were persons who were summoned to appear in court on various dates between February 2006 and December 2007, as witnesses, complainants or suspects in criminal proceedings. In conformity with article 218 of the Code of Criminal Procedure, they were asked to take the oath by placing their right hands on the Bible. Each time, they informed the authorities that they were not Orthodox Christians and preferred to make a solemn declaration instead, which they were authorised to do. The Court stated that it was thus presumed in the Code of Criminal Procedure that all witnesses were Orthodox and willing to take the oath, as reflected in the standard wording of the records of court proceedings. The Court found that requiring the applicants to reveal their religious convictions in order to be allowed to make a solemn declaration had interfered with their freedom of religion, and that the interference was neither justified nor proportionate to the aim pursued. There had therefore been a violation of article 9.[35]

To summarise, the reason for the violations of the right to freedom of belief found in the *Sofianopoulos, Folgerø, Dimitras* and *Alexandridis* judgments is not just individuals being forced to disclose their beliefs. The Court took into consideration whether the applicants had based their claim for exemption on detailed grounds, whether they had been compelled to prove they had different beliefs, and whether the authorities in question had a broad margin of appreciation when examining applications. The Court also drew attention to this issue: "the right to freedom of religion as guaranteed under the Convention excludes any discretion on the part of the State to determine whether religious beliefs or the means used to express such beliefs are legitimate."[36] In these judgments the Court extended a broad margin of appreciation to States, something which allows the authorities examining these applications to question the nature or consistency of the individuals' beliefs and, indirectly, results in them discussing the legitimacy of these beliefs. Hence, this is a kind of discretionary power which might be abused, and as a result an individual might not apply for exemption. Such a situation may naturally lead to the loss of an individual's right to exemption. This is of course a shortcoming which the Court did not envisage.[37]

The judgment in the *Sinan Işık* case in 2010 pertaining to the religion box in the identity card in Turkey is a significant judgment of the ECtHR regarding the recognition of the right of individuals not to be forced to disclose their beliefs.[38] The Court concluded that there had been a violation of article 9, contrary to the domestic courts. In this case the applicant had made an application to a domestic court to remove the word Islam on his identity card and replace it with the word Alevi. The court rejected the application, basing its decision on the opinion of the Directorate of Religious Affairs (*Diyanet İşleri Başkanlığı-Diyanet*) that Alevism cannot be accepted as an independent religion or as a sect of Islam. This judgment was ratified by the Turkish Court of Cassation on 21 December 2004, whereupon the applicant took the case to the ECtHR, asserting that the section on the identity card where a person's religion is entered compels a person to reveal his/her religious beliefs. The applicant also asserted that the *Diyanet* was not expert on the Alevi sect and that if the national court needed an opinion it could consult the Federation of Alevi Bektasi Associations. Consequently, the applicant argued there had not been a fair trial and that there had been a violation of article 6 of the Convention. Additionally, the applicant claimed the court had rejected his request on account of his being Alevi and that article 14 of the Convention had also been contravened.[39]

The Government argued that the religion box on the identity card served the purpose of ensuring public order, was in the public interest and stemmed from certain necessities connected to social needs. The Government said that there were many sects and religious orders within the religion of Islam and that to enter any of these on request would be problematic for public order and should not be done. The Government argued further that with changes made to law no. 5490, a person could request that the box on religion be left blank. It rejected claims relating to articles 6 and 14.[40]

The ECtHR firstly noted that in accordance with article 7 of law no. 5490 of 29 April 2006 that whether or not the box for religion was filled in or left blank, it still existed on the identity card. The Court further found that in the event of a person requesting that it be left blank that person was being compelled to reveal his/her belief. It made clear that States shall not attempt to learn or research persons' beliefs and that article 9 safeguarded a person's right to keep his belief secret, that is, it protected the *forum internum* dimension of this freedom. In short, the Court found a violation of article 9, saying the following:

> In any event, when identity cards have a religion box, leaving that box blank inevitably has a specific connotation. Bearers of identity cards which do not contain information concerning religion would stand out, against their will and as a result of interference by the authorities, from those who have an identity card indicating their religious beliefs. Furthermore, the fact of asking for no information to be shown on identity cards is closely linked to the individual's most deeply held beliefs. Accordingly, the Court considers that the issue of disclosure of one of an individual's most intimate aspects still arises.
>
> That situation is undoubtedly at odds with the principle of freedom not to manifest one's religion or belief. That having been said, the Court observes that the breach in question arises not from the refusal to indicate the applicant's faith (Alevi) on his identity card but from the problem of the indication—whether obligatory or optional—of religion on the identity card. It concludes therefore that the applicant may still claim to be the victim of a violation, notwithstanding the legislative amendment passed on 29 April 2006, and dismisses the Government's objection.[41]

The Court stated it could not understand the Government's argument regarding the ensuring of public order, safeguarding the public interest and ensuring social needs.[42]

In short, by placing emphasis on the fact that States cannot compel people to disclose their beliefs, the Court is stating that there can be no interference in the *forum internum* dimension of this right. Hence, since the identity card is a document individual use as part of daily life, it means they are in fact constantly having *de facto* to disclose their beliefs.

While the *forum internum* is the essential issue, a secondary matter is the State debating the legitimacy of the applicant's beliefs particularly by way of the *Diyanet*. Hence, the domestic court asked for an opinion regarding the applicant's request to have Alevi written instead of Islam from the *Diyanet*. The *Diyanet* submitted an opinion stating that Alevism should be evaluated within the scope of the Islamic religion, and not written as a separate religion in the box on the identity card. On this point, the Court stated there had been a violation of 'the State's obligation to be objective and impartial' because the individual's faith had been questioned and rejected through the *Diyanet*.[43] Indeed, the Court emphasised that States are the guarantor of pluralism, underlining its role in ensuring that beliefs behave tolerantly towards each other, stating:

> State is the ultimate guarantor of pluralism, including religious pluralism, the role of the authorities is not to adopt measures favouring one interpretation of religion over another aimed at forcing a divided community, or part of it, to come together under a single leadership against its own wishes (see *Serif v. Greece*, no. 38178/97, para. 53, ECHR 1999-IX).[44]

The Court did not find it necessary to undertake a separate examination of the case in question regarding articles 6 and 14. Since the Government did not take the case to the Grand Chamber it was finalised.

Firstly, this judgment is important in that it makes clear that solutions such as leaving the religion box blank on the identity card, from 2006, is an insufficient solution. Moreover, in practice it has been reported that registration officials have told people wanting to leave the religion box blank that they might experience difficulties in the future in fields such as military service or on applying to become a public servant.[45]

Secondly, a person's having a belief or changing that belief is defined under the *forum internum* dimension of the freedom of thought, conscience and religion. States cannot attempt to discover individuals' freedom of conscience or compel them to disclose their beliefs.[46] In other words, States have no right to interfere in this dimension of freedom. States have a duty of protecting the *forum internum* sphere of this freedom in the event of interference by third parties. In fact, the freedom of religion also includes negative rights, in that an individual has the right not to belong to a religion or practise it. Therefore, the State cannot expect a citizen to carry out anything which could very well be considered as pledging loyalty to a certain religion. This negative aspect of religious freedom also means that authorities cannot require individuals to disclose their religious beliefs, or compel them to act in a way that might indicate that they possess—or do not possess—such beliefs. State authorities cannot interfere in citizens' freedom of conscience by questioning them regarding their religious beliefs or compelling them to disclose those beliefs.[47]

Finally, another significant issue in this judgment is that the Court stated: "To construe article 9 as permitting every kind of compulsion with a view to the disclosure of religion or belief would strike at the very substance of the freedom it is designed to guarantee."[48] In other words, all manner of compulsion may not be protected within the scope of the Convention, but it does envisage authorities sometimes asking citizens to disclose information regarding their beliefs as long as this is done within States' margin of appreciation and on condition of respecting the principle of proportionality. Hence, the ECtHR did not consider some measures which necessitated the individual disclosing his beliefs as violations of article 9, by themselves, in the *Dimitras and others* case, testing these measures as to their proportionality. The fact that the Court carried out such a test means it accepts that the right not to disclose one's beliefs may be limited. This approach will result in restriction criteria being introduced by the Court where no legitimate criteria for limitation were foreseen for the *forum internum*.[49]

In sum, this judgment actually means Turkey needs to remember its obligations arising from international law. However, the fact, Turkey has still not enacted legislation, is an indicator of how seriously it takes its obligations arising from international law. At this juncture, in order to be able to comprehend the justifications made by Turkey in this case and why it has still not made the necessary reforms, it will be useful to look at the historical origins of this and examine the legal dimension in Turkey and even the decisions of the highest court in the country, the Constitutional Court.

2.3 Turkey's Obligations

In Ottoman-Turkish history the first identity card appeared after the Regulation of the Population Registration of 1881 (*Sicil-i Nüfus Nizamnamesi*), with documents called population certificates being issued.[50] These documents contained information relating to a person's religious beliefs, place of birth, place of residence, age, profession, health, marital status and, for men, their situation concerning military service.[51]

From 1906 onwards population certificates began to be replaced by 'identity booklets' (*nüfus cüzdanı*), again containing information regarding the holder's religious beliefs.[52] In 1914 a new Population Register Law was accepted, coming into effect after the founding of the Republic of Turkey in 1923.[53] This law, which remained on the statute books until 1974, also included a box for the holder's religion on identity cards.[54] The law which superseded that law in 1974 was effective until the Population Services Law was enacted in 2006. Until 2016 the religion box was not removed from identity cards until the Turkish authorities moved to identity cards with chips after the *Sinan Işık* judgment. These cards do not contain visible data pertaining to the individual's religious beliefs. However, this information is recorded in the chip and State authorities can access this information through their own systems.

The question that should be asked at this juncture is this: In spite of the Republic being established in 1923, according to article 2 of the Constitution the State is secular and although even all references to Islam have been removed from the public sphere, why is this information still being collected on identity cards?[55] Esen and Gönenç state the following on this question: "This paradox is not easy to explain, but the answer, we believe, lies in the remnants of the Ottoman Empire's Millet Sistemi (Nation System) that remained even after the declaration of the Republic."[56]

Consequently, while the official religion of the Ottoman Empire was Islam, there were people of many nations living in the country. Hence, the system was called the Nation System. Under this system, religious groups within these minorities were able to take their own decisions regarding legal and social affairs, such as marriage, divorce, inheritance and education.[57] However, with the founding of the Republic and in the Treaty of Lausanne signed in 1923, 'non-Muslim minorities', although not clearly defined in the treaty, are mentioned, and in practice the groups accepted were the Armenian Orthodox Christians, Greek Orthodox Christians and

Jews.[58] In this context, some may say that the State recorded the religious beliefs of citizens in identity cards in order to identify minority religious groups. On this point Esen and Gönenç also express the following: "The question of why the religious information continued to be included on ID cards can also be approached from a politico sociological perspective."[59]

İçduygu, Çolak and Soyarık comment thus: "[N]on-Muslim groups (Greeks, Armenians and Jews) were called Turk only in respect of citizenship but not of nationality; in terms of defining nationality they were seen as outsiders whether or not of Turkish origin, for they were not Muslim. This shows that in determining the nature of Turkish nationality, in an implicit manner, religion appeared as a significant element together with ethnicity."[60]

In short, Islam and nationality were accepted as the two main elements determining Turkish identity. In other words, the formula: 'Muslim = Turk' – 'Non-Muslim = Non-Turk' emerged.[61] In this context the concept of religion was a key element in the new Turkish identity that was intended to be created. At this juncture, Esen and Gönenç's finding is significant: "From this perspective, the preservation of religious information on ID cards during the republican era reflects one of the inherent paradoxes of Kemalist nationalism[62]; it portrayed Turkey as a staunchly secular state even while it used religion as a means to unify and mobilize the collective consciousness of the Turkish people."[63]

2.3.1 Turkish Law

As can be seen above, this has been a controversial subject ever since the founding of the Republic. Neither the Turkish Parliament nor other institutions of State have introduced, despite making some changes, any provisions that comply entirely with ECtHR judgments regarding this issue. In fact, although the *Sinan Işık* judgment and the EU accession process set forth quite plainly the international obligations, the required provisions have still not been implemented. In this context it is important to comprehend the views of Turkish law as regards this issue. With this examination it will be much clear to understand the Turkish judicial perception of secularism, the influence that the views of the *Diyanet* have on judicial bodies and whether the highest court in the country, the Constitutional Court, hands down judgments that comply with international criteria.

This topic was first the subject of a Constitutional Court judgment in 1979.[64] Two applicants wanted the word Islam to be changed on their identity cards, while a third wished the word Catholic to be changed to Armenian. The Court examining the case made the application claiming that articles 5, 13, 22, 43, 46 and 47 of law no. 1587 violated the Constitution, while the contesting court asserted that the articles in question compelled the person to reveal his belief and that in the event of a change in belief the need to ask permission from an administrative court was a violation of the constitutional principle of secularism and would be in contravention of the freedom of conscience and religion.[65] The Constitutional Court responded to these claims by stating that there was no question of any violation. Its justification for this was that the intention of the Constitution was solely for a person's religion to be revealed, not religious belief and opinions, and that there was no compulsion to reveal beliefs. In conclusion, the Court found that articles 2 and 19 of the Constitution had not been violated.[66]

It is not at all clear in this judgment on what grounds the Court distinguished between what 'religious belief and opinions' are and what one's 'religious affiliation' is. The Court stated that the ban on compulsion was only valid for 'religious belief and opinions' and that 'disclosing religious affiliation' could not benefit from Constitutional protection. Furthermore, the Court tried to ground this very superficial judgment that there had been no violation on the concept of public interest. However, this judgment does not answer the question as to how the public interest is served by an individual's religious beliefs being recorded on an identity card.[67]

The Court made a similar judgment in 1995. However, this judgment was better reasoned than the 1979 judgment and is important in understanding the stance of the Court. This case was regarding a Bahá'í requesting the term Bahá'í be entered instead of Islam. The Court stated that

> since the demographic make-up of the nation concerns the public interest, the information on 'civil status' is included in public records. The objective components of the State are the human community that constitute the country and the nation. The State needs to know the characteristics of its citizens. The State's desire to know the individuals of the community that constitutes the State and their particularities is based on public order and interest and economic, political and social needs and requirements....It cannot be construed from the article in the Constitution that states: 'No one...shall be compelled to reveal religious beliefs and convictions' that information pertaining to which religion persons are affiliated cannot be officially recorded. What the Constitution does not permit is compulsion, which concerns 'the disclosure of religious beliefs and convictions'. It is not

possible to limit the concept of 'religious beliefs and convictions' merely to 'religious information', a piece of demographic data or personal information to be written in the family register. The concept of 'religious beliefs and convictions' is not a narrow concept embodying a person belonging to this or that religion or faith, but a broad concept encapsulating many facets of religion and faith. What is prohibited by article 24 of the Constitution is not the learning of a person's religion, but their being forced to reveal their religious beliefs and convictions.[68]

This judgment is not compatible with the ECtHR's *Sofianopoulos* judgment and subsequent judgments of the Court, for the ECtHR has stated that the definition of an individual based on his religious affiliation contravenes the Convention. However, the Constitutional Court in this judgment sees religious belief as something that defines the concept of citizenship. On this point the Court demonstrates a problematic approach, for in article 2 of the Constitution it is indicated that the Republic of Turkey is a secular state. If that is the case, then accepting religious belief as a 'characteristic of a citizen' is problematic.[69]

Furthermore, the Court defined more clearly in this judgment than in its previous judgment what it meant by public interest. It based the State's requirement to determine an individual's characteristics on 'economic, political and social needs'. However, these grounds are not clearly defined. For instance, it is not clear what the relationship is between economic reasons and citizens' religious beliefs. Moreover, the use of individuals' religious beliefs for a 'political' aim in a secular state does not comply either with the principle of secularism or with the pledge to be a democratic state that respects human rights.[70] The Court also failed to address the claims of discrimination in this judgment, making no mention of the daily risk of discrimination caused by the expression of religious beliefs on the identity card different to Sunni Islam in a country that is majority Sunni Islam.[71] According to the Constitutional Court, the important question as regards the prohibition of discrimination is "not to discriminate by asking those who belong to a certain religion for information relating to their religion while not asking those who are members of a different religion. This rule is valid for everyone; hence it is general."[72] As can be seen from this sentence, the Court considers everyone being under equal threat of exposure to the risk of discrimination as sufficient to comply with the principle of equality before the law. However, the principle of equality before the law first and foremost necessitates the introduction of provisions that will remove the risk of discrimination.[73] This judgment is also open to criticism in this respect.

This judgment is also significant as regards our comprehending the Constitutional Court's perception of secularism. In this judgment the Court refers to previous judgments and lists the basic principles of secularism thus:

> a-) For religion not to be influential and dominant in affairs of State; b-)For all religions to have constitutional protection without discrimination; c-) When religion exceeds an individual's moral life and involves actions and behaviour that affect social life, restrictions shall be imposed in order to protect public order, security and public interest and no one shall be allowed to abuse or exploit religion; d-) Recognition of supervisory powers to the State as regards religious rights and freedoms in the capacity of protector of public order and rights.[74]

Only in the last of these principles are religious rights and freedoms mentioned, and this is in the context of the State's powers to impose restrictions. There are two problematic points here. Firstly, the Court evaluates its understanding of secularism on the basis of the impartiality of public authorities. The Constitutional Court tends to describe secularism on the basis of institutions, not on the basis of freedom of thought, conscience and religion. Moreover, in article 24(3) and within the scope of article 15, despite it being stated that even in exceptional circumstances people shall not be compelled to reveal their beliefs, the conclusion reached is that individuals being compelled to disclose their religious affiliations on their identity cards complies with law on account of the principle of secularism. This is problematic, both as regards the above-mentioned ECtHR judgments and as regards its interpretation of the essence of the Constitution. The fact that it considers the State may control beliefs and freedoms using the principle of secularism is not compatible with the jurisprudence of the ECtHR.[75]

The Constitutional Court did say it had opened a new page in 2012 by presenting a more 'flexible and libertarian' understanding of secularism. In this judgment the Court stated:

> A more flexible or libertarian interpretation of secularism emerges from a finding that it is a social fact in addition to being the individual dimension of religion. This understanding of secularism does not confine religion to an individual's inner world, but sees it as an important element of an individual

and collective identity, and enables it to gain social visibility. In a secular political system individual preference in religious topics and the lifestyles they shape are outside of State intervention, but under its protection. In this context, the principle of secularism is a guarantee of the freedom of religion and conscience.[76]

Contradicting previous judgments of the Court and putting emphasis on the freedom of religion and conscience is important. The Court stressed that a method of systematic review should be used in order to understand how this concept should be perceived:

> When defining this concept and setting out its components, it is clear that by means of a method of systematic review all provisions of the Constitution regarding this topic should be appraised with a holistic approach. The concept of secularism is enshrined in the preamble and articles 2, 13, 14, 68, 81, 103, 136 and 174 of the Constitution. In the articles in question secularism has been set down as a political principle defining the State's stance towards religious beliefs.[77]

However, the failure of the Court to emphasise article 24, which protects the freedom of conscience and religion, and article 15, which safeguards it even in exceptional circumstances, demonstrates that the stress referred to above is futile.[78] Hence, as in previous judgments, the Court has broadened further the approach that leads to State control and intervention on the issue of freedom of belief. While doing this it has utilised the concept of positive obligation, but it has done this without taking into consideration the freedoms of minority faith groups, on which the ECtHR has put particular stress.[79]

In this judgment the Court completely disregarded the topic of an individual's right not to disclose their beliefs, and in another individual application in 2017 it maintained its approach that nullifies the right not to reveal one's beliefs.[80]

2.3.2 Steps Taken After the Sinan Işık v. Turkey Judgment

As mentioned above the problematic judgments of the Constitutional Court defining both the concept of secularism and the scope of freedom of religion and belief are not compatible with the jurisprudence of the ECtHR. In 2010 the ECtHR handed down the *Sinan Işık* judgment. In the last ten years certain steps have been taken to enforce this judgment. For instance, in 2016, despite changes being introduced in procedures such as defining data on 'identity cards', the transferring of biometric data and so on, in the Population Services Law, no clear provision on religious information was included.[81]

In 2016, law no. 6698 'Law on the Protection of Personal Data' was enacted.[82] However, in article 6 of the law information regarding religion was considered 'data of a special kind', but it was stated that such data "could be recorded without seeking the consent of the person in question as set out in law regarding envisaged circumstances". In other words, this law did not unfortunately introduce any change concerning the religion box.

In 2016 when new identity cards with chips were introduced, although there was no box for religion on these cards, the information is still on the chip, it being stated that it would be optional to fill in the religion box on the chip.[83]

However, this does not remove the risk of discrimination mentioned in the ECtHR *Sinan Işık* judgment. Hence, information in these chips is accessible by the authorities, which increases the risk of discrimination for citizens who belong to minority faiths. And in the event of citizens leaving the box blank the possibility will emerge of a discriminatory application between those who provide religious information and those who do not.[84]

In short, the religious information is still recorded in family registers and on identity cards or on chips. It means that the State is far from implementing its obligations arising from the *Sinan Işık* judgment. For instance, as mentioned in the EU report of 2019, when it is considered that for an accused person to have the term Zoroastrian in the religion box on his identity card constituted evidence of membership of an illegal organisation, the gravity of the situation is clearly evident.[85]

2.4 Conclusion

The right not to disclose one's religious beliefs is one of the most important elements of the freedom of thought, conscience and religion, in the *forum internum* sphere, within which States do not have the right to interfere. States may not for any reason, be it secularism, public interest or on any other grounds, obstruct or impose restrictions on the exercise of this right. The relationship of this right to the principle of discrimination is also important. Hence, in countries such as Turkey, which has a population that is majority Sunni Islam, the State has a positive obligation to protect the religious beliefs of minorities. If the State does not remain impartial, these minority groups will face constant exclusion and criminal prosecution and even be subjected to political, economic and cultural discrimination.

As enshrined in articles 24 and 25 of the Turkish Constitution, individuals are protected from being compelled to disclose their convictions, as regards both belief and freedom of thought, for whatever reason or purpose. Article 15 defines this right within the category of rights that may not be interfered with even in exceptional circumstances. However, the Constitutional Court's constant interpretations of the freedom of thought, conscience and religion, which is strictly safeguarded in international law, with a problematic concept of secularism, violate the Constitution. Consequently, the above-mentioned judgments that found no interference in the right not to be compelled to disclose beliefs in the cases involving an individual's religious beliefs being recorded in family records and identity cards were in contravention of the essence of the Constitution.

In spite of the *Sinan Işık* judgment passed down in 2010, the fact that the Turkish Constitutional Court has not changed its stance on this issue merits criticism. The changes that have been made by other State authorities in light of this judgment are insufficient and not compatible with the recommendations of the Court. At the present time, although this box is no longer on identity cards, the relevant authorities can access this information via a chip system. Therefore, considering that in practice the identity card is in frequent use, the risk of individuals being subject to discrimination is very high. Especially when it is taken into account that the historical and sociological reality is one of every Turk being a Muslim, even the leaving blank of this box increases the risk of the holders being subjected to discrimination. Consequently, as stated in article 90(5) of the

Constitution, ECtHR judgments should be strictly implemented. States' positive obligations in order to prevent clear breaches are clear. Unfortunately, steps taken on this issue have been insufficient, the solution being to completely remove the box in question from the records.

Notes

1. Article 18 of the Universal Declaration of Human Rights; article 18 of the International Covenant on Civil and Political Rights (ICCPR); article 9 of the European Convention on Human Rights (ECHR); article 3 of the American Declaration of the Rights and Duties of Man; article 12 of the American Convention on Human Rights; article 8 of the African Charter on Human and Peoples' Rights.
2. B. G. Tahzib, *Freedom of Religion or Belief Ensuring Effective International Legal Protection* (The Hague/ Boston/London: Martinus Nijhoff Publishers, 1996), pp. 72–73; P. H. Halpern, 'Preliminary Report of the Proposed Study on Discrimination in the Matter of Religious Rights and Practices' (hereinafter '1954 Halpern Report'), UN Doc. E/CN.4/Sub. 2/162 (UN Publication: New York and Geneva, 1954), para. 11.
3. Tahzib, *supra note* 2, p. 73.
4. R. Reilly, 'Conscience, Citizenship, and Global Responsibilities', 23 *Buddhist-Christian Studies* (2003), pp. 117–131; K. J. Partsch, 'Freedom of Conscience and Expression, and Political Freedoms', in Louis Henkin (ed.), *The International Bill of Rights: The Covenant on Civil and Political Rights* (New York: Columbia University Press, 1981), p. 213.
5. Boyle, K., 'Freedom of Conscience, Pluralism and Tolerance: Freedom of Conscience in International Law', in Council of Europe, *Freedom of Conscience* (Strasbourg: Council of Europe Press, 1993), p. 42. Also see Partsch, *supra note* 4, p. 209.
6. Boyle, *supra note* 5, p. 42.
7. Tahzib, *supra note* 2, pp. 83–84.
8. Boyle, *supra note* 5, p. 46.
9. Partsch, *supra note* 4, pp. 210–214.
10. HRC, General Comment no. 22, 'The Right to Freedom of Thought, Conscience and Religion', UN Doc. CCPR/C/21/Rev.1/Add.4, 30 July 1993.
11. Ibid., para. 2.
12. Ibid., para. 3 (italics added).
13. *Kokkinakis v. Greece*, para. 31.

14. Ibid., para. 31; *Kustannus* Oy Vapaa Ajattelija *AB and others v. Finland*, 15 April 1996, No. 20471/92, para. 43; *Angelini v. Sweden*, 3 December 1986, No. 10491/1983, p. 41.
15. *Darby v. Sweden*, 11 April 1988, No. 11581/85, para. 51.
16. *Angelini v. Sweden*, p. 48.
17. Tahzib, *supra note* 2, p. 73.
18. J. Murdock, *Freedom of Thought, Conscience and Religion – A Guide to the Implementation of Article 9 of the European Convention on Human Rights* (Strasbourg: Council of Europe, 2007), p. 13. Also see *Van den Dungen v. the Netherlands*, 80-A Eur. Comm'n H.R. Dec. & Rep. 147 (1995), No. 22838/93, p. 147.
19. *Vereniging Rechtswinkels Ultrect v. the Netherlands*, Eur. Comm'n H.R. Dec. & Rep. 46 (1986), No. 11308/84, p. 200.
20. See, for example, *ISKCON and other v. United Kingdom*, 8 March 1994, No. 20490/92, p. 106; *Penditis v. Greece*, 9 June 1997, No. 23238/94, para. 4 (friendly settlement); *Kokkinakis v. Greece*, para. 47; *Manoussakis and others v. Greece*, 29 August 1996, No. 18748/91, para 44.
21. Article 15(2) states: "No derogation from Article 2, except in respect of deaths resulting from lawful acts of war, or from Articles 3, 4 (paragraph 1) and 7 shall be made under this provision."
22. For further information, see M. D. Evans, *Religious Liberty and International Law in Europe* (Cambridge: Cambridge University Press, 1997), p. 317; F. G. Jacobs and R. C.A. White, *The European Convention on Human Rights* (Oxford: Clarendon Press: Oxford, 2nd edition, 1996), p. 211; P. Van Dijk & G. J. H. Van Hoof, *Theory and Practice of the European Convention on Human Rights* (Deventer: Kluwer Law and Taxation, 3rd edition, 1998), p. 557.
23. *Saniewski v. Poland*, 26 June 2001, No. 40319/98.
24. Ibid., see the following link: https://hudoc.echr.coe.int/fre#{%22itemid%22:[%22001-5956%22]}, accessed 21 September 2020.
25. B. Özenç, 'İnancını Açıklamama Hakkı Açısından Türkiye Cumhuriyeti Kimlik Kartlarındaki Din Hanesi', 141 *TBB Dergisi* (2019), p. 14.
26. *Sofianopoulos v. Greece*, 12 December 2002, No. 1988/02; 1997/02; 1977/02.
27. Ibid., pp. 7–8.
28. Özenç, *supra note* 25, p. 15.
29. *Folgerø and others v. Norway*, 29 June 2007, No. 15472/02.
30. Ibid., para. 98, 100.
31. *Alexandridis v. Greece*, 21 February 2008, No. 19516/06.
32. *Dimitras and others v. Greece*, 3 June 2010, No. 42837/06, 3237/07, 3269/07, 35793/07, 6099/08.
33. *Alexandridis v. Greece*, *supra note* 31, para. 41.

34. E. Şen, '*Nüfus Cüzdanında Din Hanesinin Bulunma Zorunluluğu*', 13 August 2014, https://www.hukukihaber.net/nufus-cuzdaninda-din-hanesinin-bulunma-zorunlulugu-makale,3554.html, accessed 21 September 2020.
35. *Dimitras and others v. Greece, supra note* 32, para. 88.
36. *Manoussakis v. Greece*, 26 September 1996, No. 18748/91, para. 47; *Hasan and Chaush v. Bulgaria*, 26 October 2000, No. 30985/96, para. 78.
37. Özenç, *supra note* 25, p. 16.
38. *Sinan Işık v. Turkey*, 2 February 2010, No. 21924/05.
39. Ibid., paras. 21–32.
40. Ibid., paras. 33–35.
41. Ibid., para. 51, 52.
42. Ibid., para. 44.
43. Ibid., paras. 45–46.
44. Ibid., para. 45.
45. Norwegian Helsinki Committee, the Freedom of Belief Initiative, and Forum 18 (2019), 'Turkey UPR submission, July 2019', para. 11, https://inancozgurlugugirisimi.org/wp-content/uploads/2020/01/NHC-IOG-F18-UPR-Turkey-submission-2019-2.pdf, accessed 21 September 2020.
46. *Alexandridis v. Greece, supra note* 31.
47. Council of Europe (2020), 'Guide on Article 9 of the European Convention on Human Rights', paras. 53–54, https://www.echr.coe.int/Documents/Guide_Art_9_ENG.pdf, accessed 21 September 2020.
48. *Sinan Işık v. Turkey, supra note* 38, para. 42.
49. Özenç, *supra note* 25, p. 18.
50. 8 Şaban 1298 (5 July 1881), Irade, Suray-i Devlet 3148; also see K. H. Karpat, 'Ottoman Population Records and the Census of 1881/82–1893', 9 *Intl. J. Middle E. Stud.* (1978), pp. 237, 252; S. J. Shaw, 'The Ottoman Census System and Population', 9 *Int. J. Middle E. Stud.* (1978), pp. 325, 331.
51. Shaw, *supra note* 50, p. 331.
52. *Nüfus ve Vatandaş İşleri Müdürlüğü* (Directorate of Population & Citizenship Affairs), *Devlet-i Aliyye-i Osmaniyye Tezkiresinden Nüfus Cüzdanlarına* (From Ottoman Population Certificates to Republican Identity Booklets) 8, 12–13 (showing samples of Ottoman-Turkish identity cards) (Turkish), http://www.nvi.gov.tr/Attached/NVI/cuzdan_kitap.pdf, accessed 21 September 2020.
53. *Sicilli Nüfus Kanunu* (Population Register Law), 14 August 1330 (1914), 5. 14. Şevval 1332, 13.
54. Population Register Law, Law no. 1543, 24 February 1972.

55. Although the heading of the section on ID documents was changed from Millet (Nation) to Din (Religion), the type of information inscribed in this section remained the same.
56. S. Esen and L. Gönenç, 'Religious Information on Identity Cards: A Turkish Debate', 23 *Journal of Law and Religion* 2008, pp. 580–588.
57. S. J. Shaw, *History of the Ottoman Empire and Modern Turkey* (Cambridge: Cambridge University Press, vol. 1, 1976), p. 151.
58. See B. Oran, *Türkiye'de Azınlıklar: Kavramlar, Lozan, İç Mevzuat, İçtihat, Uygulama* (Minorities in Turkey: Conceptions, Lausanne, Domestic Regulations, Jurisprudence, Applications) (İstanbul: TESEV, 2004), pp. 36–41.
59. Esen and Gönenç, *supra note* 56, p. 583.
60. A. İçduygu, Y. Çolak and N. Soyarık, 'What is the Matter with Citizenship? A Turkish Debate', 35 *Middle East. Stud.* (1999), pp. 187, 195.
61. A. Yıldız, *Ne Mutlu Türküm Diyebilene, Türk Ulusal Kimliğinin Etno-Seküler Sınırları (1919–1938)* (İstanbul: Iletisim, 2004), p. 137.
62. L. Köker, 'National Identity and State Legitimacy: Contradictions of Turkey's Democratic Experience', in E. Ozdalga and S. Person (eds.), *Civil Society Democracy and the Muslim World* (Stockholm: Swedish Research Inst., 1997).
63. See N. Subaşı, 'Ara Dönem Din Politikaları', 93 *Toplum ve Bilim* (2002); See Esen and Gönenc, *supra note* 56, p. 584.
64. Turkish Constitutional Court, 27 November 1979, E. 1979/9, K. 1979/44.
65. H. S. Demir, *Türkiye'de Din ve Vicdan Özgürlüğü* (Ankara: Adalet, 2011), p. 112.
66. Ibid., p. 113.
67. B. Özenç, 'The Religion Box on Identity Cards as a Means to Understand the Turkish Type of Secularism', in Ö. H. Çınar and M. Yıldırım, *Freedom of Religion and Belief in Turkey* (Newcastle upon Tyne: Cambridge Scholars Publishing, 2014), pp. 101–102.
68. Turkish Constitutional Court, 21 June 1995, E. 1995/17, K. 1995/16 in Anayasa Mahkemesi Kararlar Dergisi, S. 31, Vol. 2, 1996, pp. 543–544, 548.
69. Özenç, *supra note* 67, p. 102.
70. Ibid., p. 102; Esen and Gönenç, *supra note* 56, pp. 594–597.
71. Özenç, *supra note* 67, pp. 102–103.
72. Turkish Constitutional Court, 21 June 1995, E. 1995/17, K. 1995/16, p. 547.
73. Özenç, *supra note* 67, pp. 102–103.
74. Turkish Constitutional Court, *supra note* 72, p. 546.
75. Özenç, *supra note* 67, pp. 103–104.

76. Turkish Constitutional Court, 20 September 2012, E. 2012/65, K. 2012/128, 20.9.2012, in Anayasa Mahkemesi Kararlar Dergisi, No. 50, Volume 2, 2013, p. 1443.
77. Ibid.
78. K. Altıparmak, 'Anayasa Mahkemesi ve 4+4+4: Özgürlük Hanesinde Elde Var', *Bianet*, 24 April 2013, p. 30, https://m.bianet.org/bianet/insan-haklari/146095-anayasa-mahkemesi-ve-4-4-4-ozgurluk-hanesinde-elde-var-0, accessed 21 September 2020.
79. Özenç, *supra note* 25, p. 16.
80. Turkish Constitutional Court, 8 November 2017, No. 2014/12522, para. 11.
81. See Population Services Law, Law no. 6661, 14 January 2016. Also see T. Şirin, 'Nüfus Cüzdanindaki Din Hanesi ve Zorunlu Din Dersi: Avrupa İnsan Haklari Mahkemesi İçtihadi ve Güncel Gelişmeler', https://www.academia.edu/24358896/N%C3%9CFUS_C%C3%9CZDANINDAK%C4%B0_D%C4%B0N_HANES%C4%B0_VE_ZORUNLU_D%C4%B0N_DERS%C4%B0_AVRUPA_%C4%B0NSAN_HAKLARI_MAHKEMES%C4%B0_%C4%B0%C3%87T%C4%B0H ADI_VE_G%C3%9CNCEL_GEL%C4%B0%C5%9EMELER, accessed 21 September 2020.
82. Law on the Protection of Personal Data, Law no. 6698, 24 March 2016.
83. 'Din Hanesi Kartta Yok', *Hürriyet*, 16 February 2016, https://www.hurriyet.com.tr/gundem/din-hanesi-kartta-yok-40055190, accessed 21 September 2020.
84. See Şirin, *supra note* 81.
85. European Commission (2019), 'Turkey 2019 Report', pp. 31–32, https://ec.europa.eu/neighbourhood-enlargement/sites/near/files/20190529-turkey-report.pdf, accessed 21 September 2020.

CHAPTER 3

The Military-Nation and Conscientious Objectors

Abstract The phenomenon of conscientious objection to military service raises the question of how far a State can force its citizens into obligations which may contradict individual conscience. This chapter will look at the right to conscientious objection in international law which recognises this right as legitimate expression of freedom of thought, conscience and religion. However, Turkey is the only member of the Council of Europe that does not recognise it. In this respect, this chapter will ask the following questions: Why is there no recognition of this right in Turkish law? What are the historical and sociological reasons for this lack of recognition? What are Turkey's obligations under international law? How far does Turkish law comply with these obligations?

Keywords Military • Nation • Conscientious objection/objectors • Turkey • International and domestic/national law • *Forum internum*

3.1 Introduction

Throughout history people have felt compelled to refuse to perform military service for a lot of different reasons. The most telling way to make one's opposition to war and military service clear is conscientious objection, which entails rejecting military service on the grounds of conscience based on deeply held principles of a religious, ethical, moral, philosophical, humanitarian or similar nature.

© The Author(s), under exclusive license to Springer Nature Switzerland AG 2021
Ö. H. Çınar, *Freedom of Religion and Belief in Turkey*,
https://doi.org/10.1007/978-3-030-70077-5_3

Studies have been made of this issue from many different perspectives, including historical, sociological, political and activist frames of reference.[1] It has also been taken up in human rights circles and both governmental and non-governmental organisations have taken an interest in the question of conscientious objection since 1950.[2]

Ever since the emergence of conscientious objection as a way to take a stand against war, objectors have been accused of being cowards and traitors for refusing to carry out what is seen as a fundamental national duty, to perform military service to defend the nation. This is still the case in the present day, when many objectors suffer discrimination, prosecution and imprisonment. This repression leads to many objectors being forced to flee their native countries.[3]

Furthermore, in countries like Turkey, Israel, Paraguay and Chile, where the armed forces play a dominant role, more must be done to raise the question of conscientious objection. There also needs to be public and academic debate to raise awareness of the unique status the military have in these countries, where they run their own businesses, schools, universities and hospitals.

This is particularly relevant in Turkey where conscientious objectors suffer lifelong criminal prosecutions and persecution. Not only objectors themselves, but those who support the right to conscientious objection also face severe sanctions.

This chapter will examine the current situation of the right to conscientious objection in international human rights law in order to understand Turkey's obligations. In addition, it asks the following questions in particular: Why is there no recognition of this right in Turkish law? What are the historical and sociological reasons for this lack of recognition? How far does Turkish law comply with the international obligations?

3.2   International Law Standards

At the present time the only documents that provide unequivocal recognition of the right to conscientious objection are article 10(2) of the Charter of Fundamental Rights of the European Union (EU) and article 12(1) of the Ibero-American Convention on Young People's Rights.[4] In the judicial and non-judicial mechanisms of both the United Nations (UN) and European systems the right is considered a legitimate exercise of the freedom of thought, conscience and religion.[5] The recognition of the freedom of thought, conscience and religion stems from the Universal Declaration of Human Rights (UDHR), which was adopted in 1948. Although the

UDHR does not explicitly refer to the right to conscientious objection, in article 1 it states that "[t]hey [all human beings] are endowed with reason and conscience". Article 18 also states that "[e]veryone has the right to freedom of thought, conscience and religion".[6]

It is necessary to stress certain important points relating to the recognition of the freedom of thought, conscience and religion in the UDHR. Firstly, this was a new issue for international law as this freedom had not previously been defined as an individual civil right. Secondly, in this document there is an indication of the natural state of this right, which engenders an inquiry into the individual's affiliation to the State.[7]

Additionally, although article 18 of the International Covenant on Civil and Political Rights (ICCPR) does not contain a direct reference to the right to conscientious objection, it did codify the freedom of thought, conscience and religion. Article 4 provided protection for the freedom of thought, conscience and religion by stipulating that there may be no diminution of this freedom.[8] The importance of this is that States cannot suspend these freedoms either in the event of war or in peacetime.

In addition to safeguarding the freedom of thought, conscience and religion, international mechanisms have expanded the right to conscientious objection through UN structures by various means. For instance, the Human Rights Committee (HRC) said the following apropos article 18 in a General Comment:

> Many individuals have claimed the right to refuse to perform military service (conscientious objection) on the basis that such right derives from their freedoms under article 18. In response to such claims, a growing number of States have in their laws exempted from compulsory military service citizens who genuinely hold religious or other beliefs that forbid the performance of military service and replaced it with alternative national service. The Covenant does not explicitly refer to a right to conscientious objection, but the Committee believes that such a right can be derived from article 18, inasmuch as the obligation to use lethal force may seriously conflict with the freedom of conscience and the right to manifest one's religion or belief. When this right is recognized by law or practice, there shall be no differentiation among conscientious objectors on the basis of the nature of their particular beliefs; likewise, there shall be no discrimination against conscientious objectors because they have failed to perform military service. The Committee invites States parties to report on the conditions under which persons can be exempted from military service on the basis of their rights under article 18 and on the nature and length of alternative national service.[9]

Hence, after numerous opinions had been expressed regarding individual communications inquiring as to whether a contravention of ICCPR had taken place, the HRC finally agreed that article 18 could cover the right to conscientious objection.[10] It has gone further in its two most recent views, saying that this right is safeguarded by the *forum internum* aspect of the freedom of thought, conscience and religion.[11] The fact that the HRC looked at the right to conscientious objection within the framework of the *forum internum* stresses that a State is not permitted to intervene in a person's inner being. That is, if the State appraises this right under the *forum externum*, and if the State's aims are considered legitimate, then this intervention would be deemed valid.

Moreover, the HRC has continued to expand its concluding observations, after perusing reports of States Parties regarding the right to conscientious objection, so that by September 2020 it had commented in at least 45 observations on the scope of this right.[12]

To sum up, while articles 18 of the UDHR and ICCPR expressly recognise the freedom of thought, conscience and religion, they do not mention the right to conscientious objection. Although not to be found in the UDHR, the terms 'conscientious objection' and 'conscientious objectors' are present in article 8(3)(c)(ii) of the ICCPR.[13] This article was a serious impediment that hindered the recognition of the right to conscientious objection for many years. Nevertheless, after many decades of being on the agenda of UN bodies, the right to conscientious objection is now considered a legitimate expression of freedom of thought, conscience and religion.[14]

Having observed that UN mechanisms, with which Turkey as a member of the UN which has also signed and ratified the ICCPR is obliged to comply, have a positive stance on the right to conscientious objection, it will also be beneficial to examine European mechanisms to which Turkey has signed up. The European Convention on Human Rights (ECHR) is one of the fundamental documents in Europe safeguarding the freedom of thought, conscience and religion in article 9.[15]

Article 4(3) of this Convention mentions an exception for 'compulsory military service', saying:

> For the purpose of this Article the term "forced or compulsory labour" shall not include:
> any service of a military character or, in case of conscientious objectors in countries where they are recognized, service exacted instead of compulsory military service.

Because of the above-mentioned article, the European Court of Human Rights (ECtHR) did not find any violation of article 9 of the Convention in cases brought before it by applicants specifically claiming their right to conscientious objection had been breached, until the *Bayatyan* judgment of 7 July 2011.[16] In such cases, the Court based its judgments either on article 14, which bans discrimination, or on article 3, which prohibits torture and inhuman or degrading treatment.[17] The Court's stance on this issue was seen as an anomaly when compared to the generally positive approach in international law to the right to conscientious objection, and was at variance with the Court's approach of interpreting the Convention in accordance with present-day conditions.[18]

In contrast to the European Commission of Human Rights and the ECtHR, which persisted until 2011 in holding that the Convention did not recognise the right to conscientious objection, the Parliamentary Assembly of the Council of Europe recognised the right to conscientious objection, becoming the first European body to do so, in Resolution 337[19] and Recommendation 478.[20]

Moreover, in 1987 the Committee of Ministers of the Council of Europe said in a recommendation (Recommendation No: 87/8) the following: "Anyone liable to conscription for military service who, for compelling reasons of conscience, refuses to be involved in the use of arms, shall have the right to be released from the obligation to perform such service, on the conditions set out hereafter. Such persons may be liable to perform alternative service."[21] In the same recommendation the Committee of Ministers also advised member States that did not recognise this right in their domestic law to introduce the necessary legislation.[22]

The European Parliament made a similar appeal to member States in a resolution of 13 October 1989: "Calls for the right to be granted to all conscripts at any time to refuse military service, whether armed or unarmed, on grounds of conscience, with full respect for the principles of freedom and equal treatment for all members of society."[23]

Since then the European Parliament has renewed its appeal for States to recognise the right to conscientious objection in several decisions and resolution reports.[24] Furthermore, the Resolution 1994 pointed out that the right to conscientious objection was within the framework of article 9 of the ECHR, which protects freedom of thought, conscience and religion.[25]

Until the Grand Chamber handed down its *Bayatyan* judgment on 7 July 2011, the right to conscientious objection was discussed several times in Court and Commission case-law, with the conclusion being reached that the Convention did not safeguard this right under article 9.[26] This stance was at variance with European and UN mechanisms, leading to a lack of consensus concerning the right to conscientious objection. In the *Bayatyan v. Armenia* judgment in 2011 the ECtHR established there had been a violation of article 9, for the first time evaluating the right to conscientious objection under freedom of thought, conscience and religion and ending these debates. The Court has since reached the same conclusion regarding article 9 in several other cases brought against Armenia and Turkey.[27] These judgments mean that there is now a consensus in Europe and that harmony has been established with the UN mechanisms. This new consensus will affect countries like Turkey that do not recognise the right to conscientious objection, as pressure will be put on them to recognise this right and to provide alternative service. However, the situation in Turkey will make it difficult for this right to be recognised. This will be explained in detail below.

3.3 Turkey's Obligations

In Turkey, which has been a candidate member of the EU since 2005, the army has always been a significant power. The Turkish armed forces are the second largest, after the United States of America (USA), in the North Atlantic Treaty Organization (NATO).[28] Additionally, for Turkish citizens, military service has great social, cultural, political and economic significance.

Military service is still compulsory for every male Turkish citizen when they reach 20 years of age.[29] At the present time, there are more than 500 conscientious objectors.[30][31] Of these, Osman Murat Ülke, Mehmet Tarhan and Halil Savda have served prison sentences more than once for refusing to comply with the military authorities.[32] The ECtHR made a key finding in its judgment in the case of *Ülke v. Turkey* on 5 January 2006 when stating "there is no specific provision in Turkish law governing penalties for those who refuse to wear uniform on grounds of conscience or religion".[33] The judgment continued:

> In the present case, the numerous criminal proceedings brought against the applicant, the cumulative effects of the ensuing criminal convictions and the constant alternation between prosecution and imprisonment, together with the possibility that he would face prosecution for the rest of his life, are disproportionate to the aim of ensuring that he performs his military service.

They are aimed more at repressing the applicant's intellectual personality, inspiring in him feelings of fear, anguish and vulnerability capable of humiliating and debasing him and breaking his resistance and will. The clandestine life, amounting almost to 'civil death', which the applicant has been compelled to adopt is incompatible with the punishment regime of a democratic society.[34]

The ECtHR found that article 3 of the ECHR had been violated, on account of the degrading treatment suffered by the applicant, and ordered Turkey to pay 11,000 euros in compensation. Uğur Yorulmaz, a Turkish objector, said the following regarding the ECtHR's use of the term 'civil death' to describe the situation faced by conscientious objectors in Turkey:

There is tremendous social pressure you have to face. You cannot find a job, you cannot go abroad, and you cannot get a passport. It is indeed a heavy burden when you think about all this. Then there are all the people around you—your family, your friends—that you have to face and struggle against; and you have to keep doing this every single day. All your life. Numerous times. Nothing will be over once you have made your declaration. It will continue for the rest of your life. You can't just do it and get it over with. It will stay with you.[35]

Turkey has implemented some reforms to its legislation in order to comply with the requirements of the EU accession process, but the Government has made no indication that it will accept the EU's legal and social recommendations on conscientious objection. For this reason, the EU Progress Report regarding Turkey draws attention to the Government's failure to address the issue of conscientious objection and the resulting plight of objectors and their supporters.[36]

The question that needs to be asked is this: why has the right to conscientious objection not been recognised in Turkey? Why is 'civil death' the fate of objectors? To understand why Turkey opposes the idea of conscientious objection so vehemently, it is necessary to comprehend the importance of the army in society, its influence and how militarism and nationalism have been made acceptable to the population. Before this is explored, the Turkish legal system will be examined.

3.3.1   Turkish Law

Article 72 of the Turkish Constitution of 1982 states: "national service is the right and duty of every Turk. The manner in which this service shall be performed, or considered as performed, either in the Armed Forces or in the public service shall be regulated by law."[37]

The wording of this article suggests that an alternative (civilian) service exists. However, the key part of article 72 is the following: "either in the Armed Forces or in the public service shall be regulated by law". The Law referred to here is the Military Service Act which states: "Every male Turkish citizen is obliged to perform his military service in accordance with this law."[38]

Furthermore, article 45 of the Military Penal Code states: "A person's acting in accordance with conscientious or religious scruples does not free him from criminal liability when the commission or omissions of certain acts constitute a crime."[39] This contradicts article 24 of the Constitution, which states: "Everyone has the right to freedom of conscience, religious belief and conviction." It is important to note that the Turkish Military Supreme Court and the Military Supreme Court of Appeal Departments Council have repeatedly stressed that article 45 of the Military Penal Code is the reason why the right to conscientious objection is not accepted in Turkish law.[40] Or, to put it another way, the Courts have not borne in mind article 24 of the Constitution.

Consequently, it is apparent that the above-mentioned articles of the Military Service Act and the Military Penal Code are at variance with the Constitution. Conscientious objectors are the victims, as when they refuse to carry out military service they are arraigned in a Military Court as they are deemed to be 'soldiers'. This state of affairs also contravenes International Treaties that protect the freedom of conscience, to which Turkey is a signatory.[41]

It is true that some modifications have been made to the Military Courts Act. Conscientious objectors, who are seen as draft dodgers, should now be dealt with by civil courts.[42] Hence, offences pertaining to objectors that still come under the Military Penal Code and the Turkish Penal Code will now be examined. These include *'yoklama kaçağı'* (failure to attend the 'draft examination'), *'bakaya'* (draft evasion), *'firar'* (desertion), 'persistent disobedience', deliberate avoidance of military service and inciting other servicemen to insurrection. These offences merit sentences of between one month and ten years of imprisonment (Military

Penal Code—article 63/1-a-b, article 66/1, article 87/1, article 88, article 94), depending on the seriousness of the offence.

Moreover, conscientious objectors also suffer disciplinary proceedings in addition to imprisonment. For instance, Halil Savda was put in solitary confinement for a total of more than 40 days (at intervals) for refusing to shave off his beard or wear a prison uniform.[43] Mehmet Tarhan received a ten-day solitary punishment because he shared his television with other inmates.[44]

Furthermore, any civilian who criticises the army in any way, a conscientious objector, or anybody who supports objectors and the right to conscientious objection, may be prosecuted in line with article 318 of the Turkish Penal Code which states: "1) Those who engage in activities or propaganda that would alienate the public from military service shall receive a prison sentence between six months and two years. 2) If the crime is committed through publication or broadcasting, the sentence shall increase by 50%."[45] If this article is interpreted with the 2006 Anti-Terror Law, a prison sentence of up to four and a half years could result.[46]

For instance, Halil Savda was sentenced to five months' imprisonment for issuing a press release on 1 August 2006 in support of two Israeli objectors, Amir Paster and Itzik Shabbat, who had opposed Israel's invasion of Lebanon.[47] This latter case indicates that article 318 may even be used to prosecute those who support conscientious objectors in other countries. A recent example of how article 318 is still being used against conscientious objectors and their supporters is that of Furkan Çelik, who was charged with 'alienating the public from military service'. The prosecution is based on posts on the Conscientious Objection Association's Twitter account.[48]

3.3.2 *Political, Economic, Social and Cultural Aspects of Militarism*

Conscientious objectors and those who support them encounter many legal obstacles because the country in question, Turkey, was established by the soldiers. The Turkish army is as follows: "[It] does not receive any support from democratic national will, that is organised in accordance with its own enacted laws and that establishes its own judicial mechanisms. A military establishment that determines the category of military requirements and necessities, and also the national defence requirements, that controls a huge portion of the country's budget and also can finance itself without relying on this budget, through its own foundations and companies such as Armed Forces Pension Fund Law [*OYAK*]. A military that drafts the Constitutions and provides itself with more and more immunity with each Constitutional process and that removes its own acts and laws from judicial review. An army that turns the male population of the country into figures maintaining militarism with the training applied to each and every man and by enabling the continuity of compulsory service through the abovementioned means, and that has the power to have its decisions on the problems of the country implemented through the National Security Council [*Milli Güvenlik Kurulu-MGK*]."[49]

An overwhelming majority of the population of Turkey firmly believes that if they desire to be heroes, they will have to perform their military service enthusiastically and love the army. The army is seen as a school that realises civilisation. Atatürk—the founder of the Turkish Republic—made a speech on this very subject in Konya in 1931:

> There are very few examples, in the world and in history, of the kind of union established between (our) nation and the military, made up of the nation's heroic children. We can always be proud of this national manifestation. My friends! When I talk about the military, I talk about the bright children of the Turkish nation.[50]

Atatürk frequently spoke of the relationship between the Turkish nation and the army: "The Turkish nation loves its military and considers it the guardian of its ideals."[51] What he wanted to say was that the army did not just protect the country, but was also an élite institution that constructed social life. Hence, Atatürk and his close circle made it their mission to encourage young people to become soldiers and to love the army. Since that time, the notion that 'Every Turk is born a soldier' has been taught in schools and conveyed in books.[52]

This indoctrination has led to a situation where, as Altınay notes, military service firstly has been constructed as an ahistorical reality and been installed in an unchangeable 'culture'. Secondly, military service is now perceived as a fact of life. To question the idea of military service is seen not solely as a debate around the relationship between the State and its citizens, but as challenging the very essence of Turkish culture. Thirdly, it is difficult to perceive the civilian (national) sphere independently of the military sphere. The result of this is an inextricable amalgamation of militarism with Turkish nationalism.[53]

It is also worth mentioning that women were assigned an important role: "Giving birth to soldiers!"[54] The message for men in the 'National Security Book' is also abundantly clear:

> [Military service] is the obligation to learn and practice the art of war in order to protect Turkish land, Turkish freedom and the Republic...Being a most supreme patriotic and national duty, military service familiarizes youth with the conditions of real life and educates them. *The person who does not perform military service cannot be useful to himself, his family or his country.*[55] (Italics added)

In this way, compulsory military service makes first-class citizenship exclusively masculine and attaches a certain definition to masculinity. Military service is seen as the first step on the road to manhood. It is considered a fundamental condition of manliness, to the extent that many families would prevent their daughters marrying a man if he has not performed his military service.[56]

Concerning the link between masculinity, first-class citizenship and military service, it is worthy of note that the Turkish Army considers homosexuality to be a psychosexual disorder.[57] It is now necessary to examine the experiences of homosexual conscientious objectors seeking to obtain a medical report to exempt them from military service.

3.3.3 *Homosexual Conscientious Objectors and the Unfit Report*

If a man claims that he is a homosexual and for this reason does not want to perform military service, he has to present proof of his sexual orientation to a committee at a hospital.[58] The individual may be asked to submit video or photographic evidence of him engaging in sexual relations with a partner. The individual may also be sent to a hospital for a rectal examination.[59] Individuals in such situations are also subjected to personality tests like the Minnesota Multiple Personality Inventory (MMPI). Hospitals frequently require the individual to be accompanied by a close family member, who is asked to confirm his homosexuality. Doctors ask these family members questions regarding the person's development from childhood.[60]

This procedure is in clear contravention of 'human dignity' safeguarded by article 17 of the Turkish Constitution.[61] It also violates article 8 of ECHR[62] and article 20 of the Turkish Constitution, which protect 'the freedom of private and family life'.[63]

The Turkish army has recently issued 'unfit' reports to conscientious objectors without asking for evidence. Conscientious objectors allege that this is a new tactic used by the Turkish army to marginalise well-known conscientious objectors. For instance, Halil Savda received an 'unfit' report from the Çorlu Military Hospital Medical Council for 'anti-social behaviour and lack of masculinity and Turkishness'. İskendurun Military Hospital Medical Council gave Mehmet Bal a report citing the same reasons. However, Halil Savda and Mehmet Bal have both rejected these reports.[64]

3.4 Conclusion

When Turkey's founders established the Republic, their aim was to create a new nation. With this aim in mind they transformed the State structure, constructing the new society on the concept of a military-nation. Consequently, the armed forces have always had a prominent, determining role in society.

With this objective in mind, compulsory military service has an important role to play in furthering the military-nation myth. Major-General Aytaç Yalman, a former Commander of Land Forces, referred to this role in an article, saying: "[conscription is] an indispensable guarantee of our nation-state structure...For this system endows the Turkish Armed Forces with the quality of being a part of its nation, and thus the quality of being a military-nation."[65] This is a system that is quintessentially Turkish.

Nevertheless, Turkey must endeavour to find a way to resolve this problem urgently, as the right to conscientious objection has now gained recognition from UN and European bodies, to which Turkey is a signatory, as a legitimate expression of the freedom of thought, conscience and religion. If Turkey really wishes to join the EU, then it must reform its domestic legislation to comply with international norms recognising the right to conscientious objection. Changes of this nature would raise hopes that the taboo of military-nation will be challenged and replaced by the concept of national duty.

Notes

1. See, for example, Ö. H. Çınar and C. Üsterci (eds.), *Conscientious Objection: Resisting Militarized Society* (London and New York: Zed Books, 2009); C. C. Moskos and J. W. Chambers (eds.), *The New*

Conscientious Objection: From Sacred to Secular Resistance (Oxford: Oxford University Press, 1993); R. Barker, *Conscience, Government and War: Conscientious Objection in Great Britain, 1939–45* (London: Routledge and Kegan, 1982); M. Q. Sibley and P. E. Jacob, *Conscription of Conscience: The American State and the Conscientious Objector 1940–1947* (New York: Cornell University Press, 1952); M-F. Major, 'Conscientious Objection and International Law: A Human Right?', 24 *Case Western Reserve Journal of International Law* (1992); E. N. Marcus, 'Conscientious Objection as an Emerging Human Right', 38 *Virginia Journal of International Law* (1997–1998); P. Schaffer and D. Weissbrodt, 'Conscientious Objection to Military Service as a Human Right', 9 *The Review International Commission of Jurists* (1972), pp. 33–67.
2. A statement was written by Service Civil International. This statement was then circulated by the Secretary-General of the UN in 1950, UN Doc. E/CN.4/NGO/1 Add. 1(1950) (For further information J. M. Engram, 'Conscientious Objection to Military Service: A Report to the United Nations Divisions of Human Rights', 12 *Georgia Journal of International and Comparative Law* (1982), pp. 359–399 and Major, *supra* note 1, p. 371). In 1959 Krishnaswami submitted his report which had a brief treatment of the right to conscientious objection (A. Krishnaswami, 'Study of Discrimination in the Matter of Religious Rights and Practices', UN Doc. E/CN.4/Sub. 2/200/Rev.1, New York and Geneva: UN Publication, 1960). However, the first major report was written by M. Bauer, 'Report on the Right to Conscientious Objection', Doc. 2170, Consultative Assembly of the Council of Europe, (Strasbourg: Council of Europe, 1967). For other studies in the 1960s, for example, the Church in the Modern World, 'Pastoral Constitution', *Gaudium et Spes*, no. 78–79 (Vatican: Second Vatican Council, 1965); the World Council of Churches, 'Towards Justice and Peace in International Affairs', the Fourth Assembly of Sec, II, A (Sweden: Uppsala, 1968). In the 1980s, there was another report, which was written by A. Eide—C. Mubanga-Chipoya, 'Conscientious Objection to Military Service', UN Doc. No. E/CN.4/Sub. 2/1983/30, submitted to the Sub-Commission on Prevention of Discrimination and Protection of Minorities, 36th Session, 27 June 1983.
3. U. Bröckling, *Disiplin Askeri İtaat Üretiminin Sosyolojisi ve Tarihi* (İstanbul: Ayrıntı Yayınları, 2001), p. 390; Moskos and Chambers, *supra* note 1, p. 12; *The UN Working Group on Arbitrary Detention*, 9 May 2008, Opinion No. 16/2008; Amnesty International, 'Turkey must set free conscientious objector' (London: Amnesty International, 11 January 2010); War Resisters' International, 'Turkey: Conscientious objector Mehmet Bal beaten in prison' (London: War Resisters' International, 16 June 2008).

4. Charter of Fundamental Rights of the European Union, 2000/C 364/01, OJ C 83 of 30 March 2010, adopted on 7 December 2000 and Ibero-American Convention on Young People's Rights, adopted on 10–11 October 2005, entered into force 1 March 2008. Article 10(2) of the Charter of Fundamental Rights of the European Union states: "The right to conscientious objection is recognised, in accordance with the national laws governing the exercise of this right." Article 12 of the 2008 Ibero-American Convention on Young People's Rights also states: "1-) Youth have the right to make conscientious objection towards obligatory military service. 2-) The States Parties undertake to promote the pertinent legal measures to guarantee the exercise of this right and advance in the progressive elimination of the obligatory military service. 3-) The States Parties undertake to assure youth under 18 years of age that they shall not be called up or involved, in any way, in military hostilities."
5. For further information regarding the evolution of conscientious objection, see Ö. H. Çınar, *Conscientious Objection to Military Service in International Human Rights Law* (New York: Palgrave Macmillan, 2013); M. Yıldırım, 'Conscientious Objection to Military Service: International Human Rights Law and the Case of Turkey', 5 *Religion and Human Rights* (2010), pp. 65–91; H. Takemura, *International Human Right to Conscientious Objection to Military Service and Individual Duties to Disobey Manifestly Illegal Orders* (Heidelberg: Springer, 2008); Çınar and Üsterci, *supra* note 1; D. Brett, *Military Recruitment and Conscientious Objection: A Thematic Global Survey* (Leuven and Geneva Conscience and Peace Tax International, 2006); T. Pflüger, *Professional Soldiers and the Right to Conscientious Objection in the European Union* (Brussels and London: GUE/NGL and WRI, 2008).
6. Article 18 states: "Everyone has the right to freedom of thought, conscience and religion; this right includes freedom to change his religion or belief, and freedom, either alone or in community with others and in public or private, to manifest his religion or belief in teaching, practice, worship and observance."
7. For further information on the *travaux préparatoires* of article 18 of the UDHR, see the United Nations, 'The Universal Declaration of Human Rights- An Historical Record of the Drafting Process', http://www.un.org/depts/dhl/udhr/docs_1947_1st_draftcom.shtml, accessed 21 September 2020; L. M. Hammer, *The International Human Right to Freedom of Conscience: Some Suggestions for Its Development and Application* (Dartmouth: Ashgate, 2001); A. Samnoy, *The Universal Declaration of Human Rights: Human Rights as International Consensus* (Norway: Berger Print, 1993); K. Boyle, 'Freedom of Conscience, Pluralism and Tolerance: Freedom of Conscience in International Law', in Council of

Europe, *Freedom of Conscience* (Strasbourg: Council of Europe Press, 1993); M. D. Evans, *Religious Liberty and International Law in Europe* (Cambridge: Cambridge University Press, 1997).
8. Article 4 states: "1. In time of public emergency which threatens the life of the nation and the existence of which is officially proclaimed, the States Parties to the present Covenant may take measures derogating from their obligations under the present Covenant to the extent strictly required by the exigencies of the situation, provided that such measures are not inconsistent with their other obligations under international law and do not involve discrimination solely on the ground of race, colour, sex, language, religion or social origin; 2. No derogation from articles 6, 7, 8 (paragraphs I and 2), 11, 15, 16 and 18 may be made under this provision; 3. Any State Party to the present Covenant availing itself of the right of derogation shall immediately inform the other States Parties to the present Covenant, through the intermediary of the Secretary-General of the United Nations, of the provisions from which it has derogated and of the reasons by which it was actuated. A further communication shall be made, through the same intermediary, on the date on which it terminates such derogation."
9. HRC, General Comment No. 22, 'The Right to Freedom of Thought, Conscience and Religion', UN Doc. CCPR/C/21/Rev.1/Add.4, 30 July 1993, para. 11.
10. *Godefriedus Maria Brinkhof v. the Netherlands*, 30 July 1993, No. 402/1990; *Paul Westerman v. the Netherlands*, 13 December 1999, No. 682/1996; *Yeo-Bum Yoon and Mr Myung-Jin Choi v. the Republic of Korea*, 3 November 2006, Nos. 1321/2004 and 1322/2004; *Eu-min Jung, Tae-Yang Oh, Chang-Geun Yeom, Dong-hyuk Nah, Ho-Gun Yu, Chi-yun Lim, Choi Jin, Taehoon Lim, Sung-hwan Lim, Jae-sung Lim, and Dong-ju Goh v. the Republic of Korea*, 23 March 2010, Nos. 1593 to 1603/2007.
11. *Min-Kuy Jeong et al. v. the Republic of Korea*, 27 April 2011, Nos. 1642 to 1741/2007; *Cenk Atasoy and Arda Sarkut v. Turkey*, 29 March 2012, Nos. 1853/2008 and 1854/2008.
12. Amnesty International et al., 'Third Party Intervention to the Grand Chamber of the ECtHR in the case of *Bayatyan v. Armenia*', 15 July 2010, No. 23459/03, Annex 5, pp. 21–29; R. Brett and L. Townhead, 'Conscientious Objection to Military Service', in G. Gilbert, F. Hampson and C. Sandoval, *Strategic Visions for Human Rights - Essays in Honour of Professor Kevin Boyle* (London and New York: Routledge, 2010), p. 101. Also see the official website of the Office of the United Nations High Commissioner for Human Rights, Human Rights Committee, http://www2.ohchr.org/english/bodies/hrc/sessions.htm, accessed 21 September 2020.

13. Article 8(3)(c)(ii) states: "Any service of a military character and, in countries where conscientious objection is recognized, any national service required by law of conscientious objectors."
14. For example, HRC, General Comment No. 22, *supra note* 9 and the judgment of *Yeo-Bum Yoon and Mr Myung-Jin Choi v. the Republic of Korea*, *supra note* 10.
15. Article 9 states: "1. Everyone has the right to freedom of thought, conscience and religion; this right includes freedom to change his religion or belief, and freedom, either alone or in community with others and in public or private, to manifest his religion or belief, in worship, teaching, practice and observance; 2. Freedom to manifest one's religion or beliefs shall be subject only to such limitations as are prescribed by law and are necessary in a democratic society in the interests of public safety, for the protection of public order, health or morals, or the protection of the rights and freedoms of others."
16. *Grandrath v. the Federal Republic of Germany*, 10 Y.B. Eur. Conv. on H.R. 626 (1966), No. 2299/64; *X v. Austria*, 43 Collections 161 (1973), No. 5591/72; *X v. the Federal Republic of Germany*, 9 Eur. Comm'n H.R. Dec. & Rep. 196 (1977), No. 7705/76; *Johansen v. Norway*, 44 Eur. Comm'n H.R. Dec. & Rep. 155 (1985), No. 10600/83; *A. v. Switzerland*, 38 Eur. Comm'n H.R. Dec. & Rep. 219 (1984), No. 10640/83; *Autio v. Finland*, 72 Eur. Comm'n H.R. Dec. & Rep. 245 (1990), No. 17086/90.
17. *Autio v. Finland*, 72 Eur. Comm'n H.R. Dec. & Rep. 245 (1990), No. 17086/90; *Tsirlis and Koulompas v. Greece*, 29 May 1997, Nos. 19233/91 and 19234/91; *Thlimmenos v. Greece* (GC), 6 April 2000, No. 34369/97; *Osman Murat Ülke v. Turkey*, 24 January 2006, No. 39437/98.
18. *Tyrer v. the United Kingdom*, 25 April 1978, No. 5856/72, para. 31.
19. PACE, 26 January 1967, Resolution No. 337 (1967).
20. PACE, 26 January 1967, Recommendation No. 478 (1967).
21. Council of Europe, Committee of Ministers, Recommendation No. R(87), (A) Basic Principle.
22. Ibid., preamble.
23. European Parliament, 13 October 1989, Doc. A3-15/89, 1989 O.J. (C 291) 122, 11 (1989), para. G/1.
24. For example, European Parliament, 19 January 1994, Doc. OJ (C 44) 103; European Parliament Resolution Report, 13 September 2006, 2006/2118(INI), para. 37.
25. European Parliament, 19 January 1994, Doc. OJ (C 44) 103. para. C.
26. *Bayatyan v. Armenia*, *supra note* 12.
27. *Erçep v. Turkey*, 22 November 2011, No. 43965/04; *Bukharatyan v. Armenia*, 10 January 2012, No. 37819/03; *Tsaturyan v. Armenia*, 10 January 2012, No. 37821/03; *Fethi Demirtaş v. Turkey*, 17 January 2012,

No. 5260/07; *Savda v. Turkey*, 12 June 2012, No. 42730/05; *Tarhan v. Turkey*, 17 July 2012, No. 9078/06; *Enver Aydemir v. Turkey*, 7 June 2016, No. 26012/11; *Baydar v. Turkey*, 19 June 2018, No. 25632/13; *Papavasilakis v. Greece*, 15 September 2016, No. 66899/14; *Adyan and Others v. Armenia*, 27 October 2017, No. 75604/11; *Aqhanyan and Others v. Armenia*, 5 December 2019, No. 58070/12 and 21 others; *Mushfiq Mammadov and Others v. Azerbaijan*, 17 October 2019, No. 14604/08.
28. See Statista Research Department, 'Number of military personnel in NATO countries in 2020', https://www.statista.com/statistics/584286/number-of-military-personnel-in-nato-countries/, accessed 21 September 2020.
29. The usual period of military duty in Turkey was 12 months. From June 2019 onwards it is 12 months as an officer or 6 months as a soldier. Moreover, for a payment of around 35,000 Turkish Lira (€5.261) in 2020, even this requirement can be reduced to just one month's basic training. Thus, the military service requirement is effectively different for the rich and the poor.
30. At the time of writing 562 young people had made a declaration of conscientious objection; Savaş Karşıtları, 'Türkiye'de Vicdani Reddini Açıklayanlar', https://vicdaniret.org/tarih-sirasina-gore/, accessed 21 September 2020. Since women do not have to serve in the Turkish army, their declaring themselves conscientious objectors is a gesture of support.
31. As of 23 May 2019, there are around 460,000 people who ignored their call-up papers, draft examination, draft evasion, or had applied for a delay in their service and so on (See Memurlar, 'İşte yoklama kaçağı ve bakaya kalanların sayısı', 23 May 2019, https://www.memurlar.net/haber/831785/iste-yoklama-kacagi-ve-bakaya-kalanlarin-sayisi.html, accessed 21 September 2020).
32. *Osman Murat Ülke v. Turkey*, 24 January 2006, No. 39437/98; *Savda v. Turkey*, 12 June 2012, No. 42730/05; *Tarhan v. Turkey*, 17 July 2012, No. 9078/06.
33. *Osman Murat Ülke v. Turkey*, supra note 32, 24 January 2006, para. 61.
34. Ibid., para. 62.
35. An interview with Uğur Yorulmaz, cited in Ayşe Gül Altınay, *The Myth of the Military-Nation: Militarism, Gender, and Education in Turkey* (New York: Palgrave Press, 2004), p. 110.
36. European Commission, *2018 Regular Report on Turkey's Progress Towards Accession*, 17 April 2018, p. 34.
37. 1982 Turkish Constitution, No. 2709, 7 November 1982, Official gazette dated 9 November 1982 (No. 17863). For further information see M. Yıldırım, 'The Right to freedom of Religion or Belief in Turkey –

Monitoring Report January–June 2013' (İstanbul: The Norwegian Helsinki Committee, 2013), pp. 19–22, http://inancozgurlugugirisimi.org/wp-content/uploads/2014/01/NHC-I%CC%87O%CC%88G-FoRB-Report-Eng.pdf, accessed 21 September 2020.
38. Military Service Act *(Askerlik Kanunu)*, No. 1111, 21 June 1927, Official gazette dated 12–17 July 1927 (Nos. 631–635), article 1.
39. Military Penal Code *(Askeri Ceza Kanunu)*, No. 1632, 22 May 1930, Official gazette dated 15 June 1930 (No. 1520).
40. Military Supreme Court, 4 July 1997, E. 1997/493, K. 1997/489. Also see the Military Supreme Court, 21 June 1995, E. 1995/419, K. 1995/419; Military Supreme Court, 9 April 2004, E. 2004/397, K. 2004/393; Military Supreme Court of Appeal Departments Council, 16 December 1999, E. 1999/228, K. 1999/224; Military Supreme Court, 26 December 2006, E. 2006/1547, K. 2006/1544. It should be noted that after the Bayatyan judgment, in three judgments, the Turkish Courts surprisingly recognised this right in the light of article 9 of the ECHR (*Cenk Atasoy*, 24 September 2009, Beyoğlu 2. Peace Criminal Court, E. 2009/775, K. 2009/1541; *Barış Görmez*, 16 February 2012, Isparta Military Court, E. 2012/133, K. 2012/37; *Muhammet Serdar Delice*, 24 February 2012, Malatya Military Court, E. 2012/98, K. 2012/40).
41. Turkey signed the UDHR on 6 April 1949, Law on the Adoption of the Universal Declaration of Human Rights, No. 9119, Official gazette dated 27 May 1949 (No. 7217). Turkey signed the ICCPR on 15 August 2000 and ratified it on 4 June 2003, Law on the Adoption of the ICCPR, No. 4868, Official gazette dated 21 July 2003 (No. 25175). Turkey also signed the ECHR on 20 March 1952 and ratified it on 10 March 1954, Law on the Adoption of the ECHR, No. 6366, Official gazette dated on 19 March 1954 (No. 8662).
42. Law on the Organisation and Procedures of Military Courts *(Askeri Mahkemeler Kuruluşu ve Yargılama Usulü Kanunda Degişiklik Yapılmasına Dair Kanun)*, Amended Law No. 5530, 29 June 2006, Official gazette dated 5 July 2006 (No. 26219), article 4. Also see a statement of the Director of Criminal Justice Department of the Minister of Justice dated 03 July 2008, No. B.03.0.CİG.0.00.00.05-647.03-105-2007/775/38574.
43. Hülya Üçpınar, 'The criminality of conscientious objection in Turkey and its consequences', in Çınar and Üsterci, *supra note* 1, p. 246.
44. Zana Yavuz, 'Tarhan'a Televizyon Cezası', *Akşam Gazetesi*, 19 February 2006, http://www.savaskarsitlari.org/arsiv.asp?ArsivTipID=5&ArsivAnaID=31453, accessed 21 September 2020.

45. The new Turkish Penal Code *(Türk Ceza Kanunu)*, Amended Law No. 5237, 26 September 2004, Official gazette dated 12 October 2004 (No. 25611), article 318.
46. All sentences to be increased by half.
47. 'Vicdani retçi Halil Savda'ya hapis', *Birgün*, 3 June 2008, http://www.savaskarsitlari.org/arsiv.asp?ArsivTipID=5&ArsivAnaID=45696, accessed 21 September 2020. Also see Initiative for Freedom of Expression, *Article 318 File TPC 318: Alienating the people from Military Service* (İstanbul: Initiative for Freedom of Expression, 2007), http://www.antenna-tr.org/exel/son%20i.doc, accessed 21 September 2020.
48. Brett, *supra note* 5, p. 21.
49. Osman Can, 'Conscientious Objection and the Turkish Constitution', in Çınar and Üsterci, *supra note* 1, p. 231.
50. T. Parla, *Atatürk'ün Söylev ve Demeçleri*, Volume 2 (Istanbul: Iletisim Press, 1991), pp. 169–170, cited in Altınay, *supra note* 35, p. 123.
51. Ibid.
52. İ. H. Vural, *Vatandaşlık ve İnsan Hakları Eğitimi* (İstanbul: Serhat Publishing Company, 1999); F. Güventürk, and T. Olcaytu, *Lise ve Dengi Okulları İçin Milli Güvenlik Bilgileri* (İstanbul: Okat Yayınevi, 1972); Milli Eğitim Bakanlığı, *Milli Güvenlik Bilgileri I* (İstanbul: Okat Yayınevi, 1965).
53. A. G. Altınay, 'Refusing to Identify as Obedient Wives, Sacrificing Mothers and Proud Warriors' in Çınar and Üsterci, *supra note* 1, p. 89; A. G. Altınay, 'Eğitimin Militarizasyonu: Zorunlu Milli Güvenlik Dersi' in A. İnsel and A. Bayramoğlu (eds.), *Bir Zümre, Bir Parti Türkiye'de Ordu* (İstanbul: Birikim Yayınları, 2004), p. 188.
54. A. G. Altınay, 'Ordu-Millet-Kadınlar: Dünyanın İlk Kadın Savaş Pilotu Sabiha Gökçen', in A. G. Altınay (ed.), *Vatan Millet Kadınlar* (İstanbul: İletişim Yayınları, 2004), pp. 279–287.
55. *Milli Güvenlik Bilgisi* (İstanbul: Milli Eğitim Basımevi, 1998) p. 20, cited in A. G. Altınay, 'Refusing to Identify as obedient wives, sacrificing mothers and proud warriors', in Çınar and Üsterci, *supra note* 1, p. 90.
56. E. Siclair-Webb, '"Our Bulent is now a Commando": Military Service and Manhood in Turkey', in M. Ghoussoub and E. Sinclair- Webb (ed.), *Imagined Masculinities: Male Identity and Culture in the Modern Middle East* (London: Saqi Books, 2000), pp. 65–91. Also see P. Selek, *Sürüne Sürüne Erkek Olmak* (İstanbul: İletişim Yayınları, 2009).
57. For further information, see Amnesty International Turkey, 'Conscientious objector Mehmet Tarhan is a Prisoner of Conscience and must be released now!', AI Index: EUR 44/036/2005 (Public), News Service No: 338, 9 December 2005. Also see A. Biricik, 'Rotten Report and Reconstructing Hegemonic Masculinity in Turkey', in Çınar and Üsterci, *supra note* 1, p. 116.

58. While the Turkish Armed Forces does not explicitly ban homosexuality, article 17-D(4) of the Turkish Armed Forces' Health Eligibility Regulations' Supplementary Illnesses and Defects List *(Türk Silâhlı Kuvvetleri Sağlık Yeteneği Yönetmeliği'nin Eki olan 'Hastalık ve Arızalar Listesi)* states that if a person has a clear 'Sexual Identity and Psychosexual Disorder' that affects his entire life, this must be documented in order to identify any potentially negative effects on military discipline. The Turkish Military Penal Code also states that any soldier who engages in *'gayri tabii mukarenet'* (unnatural behaviour) will be discharged and lose his rank (Turkish Military Penal Code, article 153). The enacted Turkish Armed Forces Disciplinary Law also dismisses from the armed forces any soldier guilty of practising unnatural behaviour (Turkish Armed Forces Disciplinary Law *(Türk Silahli Kuvvetleri Disiplin Kanunu)*, Law No. 6413, 31 January 2013, Official gazette dated 16 February 2013 (No. 28561), article 20(1)(ğ)). For further information, see Alp Biricik, 'Diagnosis... Extremely Homosexual: (Re)Constructing Hegemonic Masculinity through Militarised Medical Discourse in Turkey', Master Dissertation (Budapest: Central European University, 2006), p. 7 and Biricik, *supra* note 57, pp. 112, 116 (footnote 4).
59. Biricik, *supra note* 57, pp. 113. Also see Lambda–İstanbul, *Ne Yanlışız Ne de Yalnızız: Bir Alan Çalışması, Eşcinsel ve Biseksüellerin Sorunları* (İstanbul: Berdan Matbaacılık, 2006).
60. Kaos GL, 'GATA'dan Eşcinsellere Yeni Psikolojik İşkence: Aile Görüşmesi', 3 March 2012, http://www.kaosgl.com/sayfa.php?id=10733, accessed 21 September 2020.
61. Article 17 states: "Everyone has the right to life and the right to protect and improve his/her corporeal and spiritual existence. The corporeal integrity of the individual shall not be violated except under medical necessity and in cases prescribed by law; and shall not be subjected to scientific or medical experiments without his/her consent. No one shall be subjected to torture or mal-treatment; no one shall be subjected to penalties or treatment incompatible with human dignity."
62. Article 8 states: "1. Everyone has the right to respect for his private and family life, his home and his correspondence; 2. There shall be no interference by a public authority with the exercise of this right except such as is in accordance with the law and is necessary in a democratic society in the interests of national security, public safety or the economic well-being of the country, for the prevention of disorder or crime, for the protection of health or morals, or for the protection of the rights and freedoms of others." Also see *L. and V. v. Austria* and *S.L. v. Austria*, 9 January 2003, Nos. 39392/98 and 39829/98 and No. 45330/99; *Dudgeon v. United Kingdom*, 22 October 1981, No. 7525/76.

63. Article 20 states: "Everyone has the right to demand respect for his/her private and family life. Privacy of private or family life shall not be violated."
64. See 'Vicdani Retçi Mehmet Bal Başına Gelenleri Anlattı', *Bianet*, 26 June 2008, https://m.bianet.org/bianet/ifade-ozgurlugu/107902-vicdani-retci-mehmet-bal-basina-gelenleri-anlatti, accessed 21 September 2020. Also see H. Savda, 'Savda: Çürük olan militarist kurum, yapı ve zihniyettir', *Savaş Karşıtları Gündem Arşivi*, 17 July 2008; B. Kenter, 'Anti-sosyal kişilik bozukluğu teşhisi', *Savaş Karşıtları Gündem Arşivi*, 24 December 2008; Anarşist Perspektif, 'Çürük Değil, Vicdani Ret', 28 November 2010, http://anarsistperspektif.blogspot.com/2010/11/, accessed 21 September 2020.
65. Mehmet Ali Kışlalı, 'Postmodern Ordu ve TSK', *Radikal*, 20 Ocak 2007, p. 14.

CHAPTER 4

Unresolved Issue: Compulsory Religious Education

Abstract The question of religious education has been debated in Turkey since it was established in 1923. However, with Turkey's commencement of the accession process towards becoming a full member of the European Union, this debate has intensified, and after the European Court of Human Rights' judgments on Turkey, obligations arising from international law have become more impellent. Therefore, this chapter will explore the history of religious education in Turkey, followed by an in-depth look at the current legal situation of compulsory religious instruction in Turkey. It will also examine the Turkish court judgments.

Keywords Compulsory religious education • Right to education • Turkey • International and domestic/national law • *Forum internum and externum*

4.1 Introduction

The subject of religious education has been a topic of debate ever since Turkey was founded in 1923. This discussion has focused on the links between religion, the State, society in general and the individual. After the European Court of Human Rights' (ECtHR's) landmark judgments in *Hasan and Eylem Zengin* and *Mansur Yalçın and others*, Turkey's obligations arising from international law have attracted closer attention. Since Turkey began the process of joining the European Union (EU), debate around this issue has escalated, with a wide variety of views being put

© The Author(s), under exclusive license to Springer Nature Switzerland AG 2021
Ö. H. Çınar, *Freedom of Religion and Belief in Turkey*,
https://doi.org/10.1007/978-3-030-70077-5_4

forward. While some commentators call for compulsory religious education, others believe there should be no religious education in schools, and others call for classes to be optional.[1]

In this chapter, the issue will be studied under two headings. Firstly, the question of how compulsory religious education is framed in international human rights documents will be examined and the attitudes of international mechanisms studied. The relevant case law of the ECtHR will be looked at, in particular the *Zengin* and *Yalçın* judgments. In the second part of the study, the history of religious education in Turkey will be examined, followed by an in-depth look at the current legal situation of compulsory religious instruction in Turkey. Turkish court judgments will be scrutinised as part of this study, with a particular focus on the effects of the *Zengin* and *Yalçın* judgments on Turkish jurisprudence.

4.2 International Law Standards

International documents contain many provisions that safeguard the rights of parents and children concerning religious education. Article 2 of protocol 1 of the European Convention on Human Rights (ECHR), for example, states:

> No person shall be denied the right to education. In the exercise of any functions which it assumes in relation to education and to teaching, the State shall respect the right of parents to ensure such education and teaching in conformity with their own religions and philosophical convictions.

Furthermore, paragraph 4 of article 18 of the International Covenant on Civil and Political Rights (ICCPR) requires states to respect parents' freedom to have religious and moral education for their children that accords with their beliefs.

Article 26(3) of the Universal Declaration of Human Rights (UDHR) underlines parents' right to have a say in their children's education. The United Nations (UN) Convention on the Rights of the Child also puts the rights of the child first. Article 14 states:

> 1-) States Parties shall respect the right of the child to freedom of thought, conscience and religion; 2-) States Parties shall respect the rights and duties of the parents and, when applicable, legal guardians, to provide direction to the child in the exercise of his or her right in a manner consistent with the

evolving capacities of the child; 3-) Freedom to manifest one's religion or beliefs may be subject only to such limitations as are prescribed by law and are necessary to protect public safety, order, health or morals, or the fundamental rights and freedoms of others.

Apart from international conventions, international bodies like the UN Human Rights Committee (HRC), the Parliamentary Assembly and the Committee of Ministers of the Council of Europe have stated their views on this topic.

The HRC found that paragraph 4 of article 18 of the ICCPR had been contravened in the case of *Leirvåg and ors v. Norway* because children had not been able to opt out of compulsory religious education that was not of an objective or neutral character.[2] In its case, the HRC concluded that

> the difficulties encountered by the authors, in particular the fact that Maria Jansen and Pia Suzanne Orning had to recite religious texts in the context of a Christmas celebration although they were enrolled in the exemption scheme, as well as the loyalty conflicts experienced by the children, amply illustrate these difficulties. Furthermore, the requirement to give reasons for exempting children from lessons focusing on imparting religious knowledge and the absence of clear indications as to what kind of reasons would be accepted creates a further obstacle for parents who seek to ensure that their children are not exposed to certain religious ideas. In the Committee's view, the present framework of CKREE [Christian Knowledge and Religious and Ethical Education], including the current regime of exemptions, as it has been implemented in respect of the authors, constitutes a violation of article 18, paragraph 4, of the Covenant in their respect.[3]

The HRC continued by saying that "[i]n accordance with article 2, paragraph 3 (a), of the Covenant, the State party is under an obligation to provide the authors with an effective and appropriate remedy that will respect the right of the authors as parents to ensure and as pupils to receive an education that is in conformity with their own convictions. The State party is under an obligation to avoid similar violations in the future."[4]

Furthermore, the HRC emphasised that those who are affiliated to minority faiths should not be compelled to reveal their beliefs to gain the right to opt out of religious education.[5] The HRC also stressed in its General Comment no. 22 that classes on religious culture and ethics could meet the terms of article 18 as long as they were neutral and objective. It stated:

The Committee is of the view that article 18.4 permits public school instruction in subjects such as the general history of religions and ethics if it is given in a neutral and objective way. The liberty of parents or legal guardians to ensure that their children receive a religious and moral education in conformity with their own convictions, set forth in article 18.4, is related to the guarantees of the freedom to teach a religion or belief stated in article 18.1. The Committee notes that public education that includes instruction in a particular religion or belief is inconsistent with article 18.4 unless provision is made for non-discriminatory exemptions or alternatives that would accommodate the wishes of parents and guardians.[6]

As for the Parliamentary Assembly of the Council of Europe, its recommendation no. 1720 in 2005 read as follows:

The Assembly also recommends that the Committee of Ministers encourage the governments of member states to ensure that religious studies are taught at the primary and secondary levels of state education, on the basis of the following criteria in particular:
    the aim of this education should be to make pupils discover the religions practised in their own and neighbouring countries, to make them perceive that everyone has the same right to believe that their religion is the "true faith" and that other people are not different human beings through having a different religion or not having a religion at all;
    it should include, with complete impartiality, the history of the main religions, as well as the option of having no religion.[7]

All in all, it is apparent that the above-mentioned international conventions and the manner in which international bodies interpret them make absolutely clear that if schools are going to provide compulsory religious education, this education must include a non-discriminatory exemption process if only one religion is to be taught.[8] This education should also be of an objective, pluralist and critical nature. It is also important to examine the judgments of the ECtHR on this question, to understand if any breaches of the ECHR have been found.

4.2.1   European Court of Human Rights' Case Law

The ECtHR has concluded, in cases such as *Angelini v. Sweden, Saniewski v. Poland and Folgerø and others v. Norway*, that compulsory religious education is acceptable in schools, with the proviso that no single belief is taught.[9] In these judgments, the importance of lessons being objective, critical and pluralist is stressed.

In one case, that of *Grzelak v. Poland*, the Court concluded that an ethics class which an agnostic family had asked to be provided for their child was sub-standard.[10] The ECtHR declared that "the Court is not satisfied that the difference in treatment between non-believers who wished to follow ethics classes and pupils who followed religion classes was objectively and reasonably justified and that there existed a reasonable relationship of proportionality between the means used and the aim pursued. The Court considers that the State's margin of appreciation was exceeded in this matter as the very essence of the third applicant's right not to manifest his religion or convictions under article 9 of the Convention was infringed."[11] Consequently, the Court found violations of article 14 read together with article 9 of the ECHR.[12]

In a landmark judgment in the *Hasan and Eylem Zengin* case, the ECtHR examined compulsory religious classes in Turkey.[13] In this case, the applicant-Mr Hasan Zengin-, an Alevi, had requested exemption from his daughter -Miss Eylem Zengin- from Religious Culture and Ethics classes. In his application to the Turkish education authorities, he had mentioned his rights concerning his child's education safeguarded by international documents such as the UDHR, adding that compulsory religious education violated the principle of secularism.[14] After Mr Zengin's application was rejected, he appealed to the İstanbul Administrative Court, which threw out the case on 28 December 2001, declaring:

> Article 24 of the Constitution has established that religious culture and ethics are among the compulsory subjects taught in primary and secondary schools, and section 12 of Law no. 1739 [states] that religious culture and ethics are among the compulsory subjects taught in primary and upper secondary schools of the equivalent level. In this context, the dismissal of the applicant's request is not contrary to the law.[15]

Once the Council of State had ratified the judgment on 14 April 2003, meaning all domestic remedies had been exhausted, the applicant went to the ECtHR. In his submission Mr Zengin emphasised two points: firstly, that religious education in Turkish schools only taught Sunni Muslim beliefs, rejecting the Alevi faith, and, secondly, that it was not for a secular state to make decisions on religion.[16]

The Court began by examining the character of the education to establish whether it was 'objective, critical and pluralist'. It then emphasised that it was important to understand whether the Turkish education system guaranteed respect for the beliefs of parents.

The Court arrived at the following judgment after scrutinising years 4, 5, 6, 7, 8 and 9 in the Religious Culture and Ethics classes:

> As to the textbooks used in the context of these classes, examination shows that they are not limited to transmitting information on religions in general; they also contain texts which appear to provide instruction in the major principles of the Muslim faith and provide a general overview of its cultural rites, such as the profession of faith, the five daily prayers, Ramadan, pilgrimage, the concepts of angels and invisible creatures, belief in the other world, etc.
>
> Equally, pupils must learn several suras from the Koran by heart and study, with the support of illustrations, the daily prayers and sit written tests for the purpose of assessment.
>
> Thus, the syllabus for teaching in primary schools and the first cycle of secondary school, and all of the textbooks drawn up in accordance with the Ministry of Education's decision no. 373 of 19 September 2000, give greater priority to knowledge of Islam than they do to that of other religions and philosophies...
>
> Moreover, the question arises whether the priority given to the teaching of Islam may be considered as remaining within acceptable limits for the purposes of article 2 of Protocol No. 1. In fact, given the syllabus and textbooks in question, it may reasonably be supposed that attendance at these classes is likely to influence the minds of young children. It is therefore appropriate to examine whether the information or knowledge in the syllabus is disseminated in an objective, critical and pluralist manner...
>
> As the Government have recognised, however, in the "religious culture and morals" lessons, the religious diversity which prevails in Turkish society is not taken into account. In particular, pupils receive no teaching on the confessional or ritual specificities of the Alevi faith, although the proportion of the Turkish population belonging to it is very large. As to the Government's argument that certain information about the Alevis was taught in the 9th grade, the Court, like the applicants, considers that, in the absence of instruction in the basic elements of this faith in primary and secondary school, the fact that the life and philosophy of two individuals who had a major impact on its emergence are taught in the 9th grade is insufficient to compensate for the shortcomings in this teaching...

In the light of the above, the Court concludes that the instruction provided in the school subject "religious culture and ethics" cannot be considered to meet the criteria of objectivity and pluralism and, more particularly in the applicants' specific case, to respect the religious and philosophical convictions of Miss Zengin's father, a follower of the Alevi faith, on the subject of which the syllabus is clearly lacking.[17]

Concerning the second question, the Court concluded that

> the Court considers that the exemption procedure is not an appropriate method and does not provide sufficient protection to those parents who could legitimately consider that the subject taught is likely to give rise in their children to a conflict of allegiance between the school and their own values. This is especially so where no possibility for an appropriate choice has been envisaged for the children of parents who have a religious or philosophical conviction other than that of Sunni Islam, where the procedure for exemption is likely to subject the latter to a heavy burden and to the necessity of disclosing their religious or philosophical convictions in order to have their children exempted from the lessons in religion.[18]

In sum, the Court found, therefore, that the religious education provided was not objective, pluralist or critical, and that the lessons in question did not respect the applicants' beliefs. The Court also found the declaration of faith required from parents to gain exemption for their children to be in contravention of the prohibition on disclosure of faith. It also found that there was no decision-making process to deal with requests for exemption, with the decision being left to the school administration. The Court consequently found a violation of article 2 of protocol no. 1 of the ECHR.[19] The Court considered that there was no separate issue to address under article 9.[20]

In the case of *Mansur Yalçın and others v. Turkey*, the Court also concluded that there had been a violation of article 2 of protocol no. 1 of the ECHR, while on the same grounds mentioned in the *Zengin* judgment it found no separate question with regard to article 9.[21]

Following the Turkish Government's lack of concrete action after these judgments had been handed down, the Committee of Ministers of the Council of Europe called on Turkey on several occasions to draft new legislation in domestic law and the education system in order to meet its obligations arising from article 2 of protocol no. 1 of the Convention.[22] Article 46 of the ECHR makes it clear that the Turkish National Assembly has a responsibility to make changes to domestic legislation that contravenes the ECHR.[23]

The Turkish Government notified the Committee of Ministers that it had arranged for 'Alevi workshops' to be held in June 2009 and January 2010. At these events, a decision was taken to set up a commission to review the content of religious classes by the Ministry of National Education. The Ministry subsequently sent a CD to the Committee of Ministers containing the changes that it intended to make to Religious Culture and Ethics classes.[24]

A report was compiled after the above-mentioned workshops were held, and submitted to the Prime Minister's office. In the report was the following passage:

> In order for the education and instruction curriculum that provides opportunities for all citizens according to their wishes as laid down in article 24 of the Constitution to be more effective, the necessary technical work should be launched by the relevant branches of the Ministry of National Education in order for all faith groups, first and foremost Alevis, to benefit from these lessons....The current state of religious classes should be revised. The curriculum should be prepared at an equal distance from all spheres of belief.[25]

In 2015, the Turkish Government notified the Committee of Ministers that it would set up a working group that involved the Ministry of Justice and the Presidency of Religious Affairs, academics from a variety of backgrounds and representatives of NGOs, as part of its action plan. This working group was to be coordinated by the Ministry of National Education. The Government stated that it would decide on which steps were required to implement the ECtHR judgments after receiving a report compiled by the working group. However, since then no information has emerged regarding who was involved in the working group, how it functioned or the report.[26]

Hence, although these action plans were well received, at the time of writing fundamental problems still exist:

> The Sunni Islamic perspective remains dominant in the syllabus; Atheism, agnosticism, and deism are presented under the heading 'Other Approaches', and Islamic apologia are presented alongside them; One of the goals of the syllabus is listed as the adoption by the students of 'national values', however these values are not presented in a way that conveys the religious and other diversity in Turkey; There is no provision for a non-discriminatory

mechanism for exemption from the RCE [Religious Compulsory Education] course. Currently, only Christian and Jewish students are able to take advantage of the exemption, by showing their religious identities as recorded in the religion category on their identity documents. Students who want to benefit from the right to exemption, but who do not belong to these religions, cannot benefit from this right and are forced to participate in the course and earn passing grades on the exams. Christian refugee students whose identity cards do not have a religion field are also forced to take the RCE course; Students who are exempted from the RCE courses are subjected to an unequal calculation of their scores on the High School Placement System test relative to other students.[27]

To understand this situation, it is essential to examine the history of compulsory religious education in Turkey and its legal background.

4.3 Turkey's Obligations

4.3.1 The History of Religious Education in Turkey

Turkey was established after the collapse of the Ottoman Empire.[28] During the Ottoman period, religious schools (*medrese*), ordinary schools (*mektep*) and foreign schools for non-Muslims had existed. The subjects taught at these schools were very different. In religious schools Muslims learnt about *tecvid* (recitation of the Koran) and *ilm-i hal* (knowledge of circumstances). Foreign schools had been established with backing from countries such as Britain, France and the United States of America (USA).[29]

Soon after, the founding of Turkey vocational religious schools (*İmam Hatip*) and a Faculty of Theology were set up, with the Ministry of National Education being given control of all schools.[30] This was enshrined in article 80 of the Constitution of 1924, which stated, "All manner of education is free and legal under the supervision and control of the Government."

Primary school pupils began to have religious instruction of between one and two hours a week in 1924. This continued until 1931 when religious education stopped in primary schools. As for secondary schools and high schools, religious education also started in 1924, but ended in 1927. Turkish schools did not provide any religious education until 1948, except for village primary schools, which continued to have religious instruction until 1939.[31]

Until the second National Education Council in 1943, the subject of the reintroduction of religious education was not mentioned. At the Council, there was a debate along these lines: "the development of moral education in schools and its inclusion in the curriculum of primary schools in order for these tenets to be realized." The term 'moral education' used in these debates was a euphemism for religious education.[32]

There was also debate in the Turkish Parliament, with some MPs calling for religious education to be reintroduced in schools. They asserted that secularism should not be seen as an obstacle to religious belief. Proponents of the reintroduction of religious education believed that it would be a bulwark against the rise of communism, which was seen as a threat at the time.[33]

Recep Peker, who held the position of Prime Minister from 1946 to 1947, said the following regarding the reintroduction of compulsory religious instruction: "to consider the substitution of a slowly developing Islamic law in order to protect society from the social poison called communism is to assume that a lethal venom can be treated with an equally lethal poison."[34]

There were some prominent opponents of the reintroduction of religious education. Hasan Ali Yücel, who was Education Minister from 1938 to 1946, said: "Religious education is for those who have reached puberty. It is disrespectful to freedom of conscience to give religious lessons to primary school pupils and to some secondary school pupils who are intelligent but have yet to reach puberty."[35]

The decision to reintroduce religious instruction in primary schools was taken, after a long debate, on 19 February 1948. In 1949, religious education classes began, with the introduction of a regulation regarding pupils in years 4 and 5 having two hours of classes a week, contingent on the consent of parents. In 1950, parents were permitted to apply for exemption from religious instruction for their children. In 1951, religious instruction was also introduced to teacher training schools and 'village institutes'.[36,37]

Religious education classes were introduced to the syllabus of secondary schools in 1956, contingent on parental consent. Students who attended religious education classes once a week in the first and second classes had to demonstrate success at the end of the school year in order to progress to the next class.[38]

The Constitution of 1961, which was drafted after the military coup of 1960, grounded religious education in its text. Paragraph 4 of article 19 states, "Religious education and instruction is dependent on the wishes of the parents or the legally appointed guardians of minors." High school curriculums introduced one-hour religious education classes for the first two years after parents requested it in 1967. After the military coup of 1971, the subject of religious education was back on the agenda, with the secondary part of *İmam Hatip* schools being closed down. However, in 1974, morality classes were brought in and a year later religious instruction of one hour a week became part of the curriculum of the final two years of primary schools, all three years of secondary schools and the first two years in high schools. In 1976, religious education began in year 3 in high schools.[39]

After the military coup of 1980, religious education was one of the most controversial topics of discussion. The initial draft of the 1982 Constitution incorporated the provision in article 19 of the 1961 Constitution, but of the 15 members of the drafting commission, 13 objected to the principle of parental consent, demanding that religious and moral education be made compulsory in primary and secondary schools. Consequently, article 24 of the current Constitution was framed to reflect this view.[40] The leader of the Junta, Kenan Evren, who later became the President of Turkey, believed that the State should retain control of religious education.[41] Hence, the decision of the National Security Council regarding this issue was proclaimed thus on 24 July 1981:

> By taking this new decision, religious education will be introduced in every primary, middle and high school on a compulsory basis. Consequently, our pupils will receive religious education from state schools. In the majority of Western countries religious education is given by schools. In fact, compulsory religious education in schools is compatible with secularist principles. In this matter Atatürk stated: 'Religion must be taken out from the hands of ignorant people, and the control should be given to the appropriate people'. For these reasons, we will introduce compulsory religious education in our schools.[42]

When introduced in 1982 these courses bore the title of 'religion and ethics knowledge', but in October of the same year, this was changed to 'religious culture and ethics knowledge'. While the name changed, the content of the instruction given was the same, comprising the Sunni version of Islam, in spite of the name suggesting a broader perspective. Until

July 1990, when Christian and Jewish children were granted exemption, these classes were even compulsory for non-Muslims.[43]

In 1991, two hours of 'Religious Culture and Ethics' were included in the curriculum of high schools. From the year 2000 to 2017, years 4, 5, 6, 7 and 8 of primary schools received two hours a week of compulsory religious instruction, and students at secondary schools received one hour a week during all 4 years.[44]

Currently, students have compulsory religious education for two hours a week from year 4 to year 12 (9 years). Furthermore, the Board of Education and Discipline took a decision on 19 September 2000, issuing a list of the prayers that were to be learned by heart in these lessons. This by itself conveys an idea about what is taught in these classes.[45]

Certain changes were made to the curriculum in 2005 after parents complained,[46] but as these sentences are being written in 2020, complaints concerning what is taught in classes continue to be made.

4.3.2 Turkish Law

As has been outlined above, the issue of religious instruction in schools has been a contentious question in Turkey since it was founded nearly a hundred years ago. It is worthy of note that the secular structure in Turkey was not established until 1937. Article 2 of the present Constitution, dated 1982, states:

> The Republic of Turkey is a democratic, *secular* and social State governed by the rule of law; bearing in mind the concepts of public peace, national solidarity and justice; respect for human rights; loyalty to the nationalism of Atatürk, and based on the fundamental tenets set forth in the Preamble. (Italics added)

Article 24, paragraph 4 of this Constitution states the following concerning compulsory religious education:

> Education and instruction in religion and ethics shall be conducted under State supervision and control. Instruction in religious culture and moral education shall be compulsory in the curriculum of primary and secondary schools. Other religious education and instruction shall be subject to the individual's own desire, and in the case of minors, at the request of their legal representatives.

According to a report issued by the State Planning Organisation in 1983, the article cited above was drafted for the purpose of safeguarding national integrity.[47] Furthermore, the terms religion and ethics were expressed separately, thus 'instruction in religious culture and moral education'. The ECtHR judgment in the case of *Campbell and Cosans* explained the difference between instruction and education in the following way:

> [T]he education of children is the whole process whereby, in any society, adults endeavour to transmit their beliefs, culture and other values to the young, whereas teaching or instruction refers in particular to the transmission of knowledge and to intellectual development.[48]

In the article in question, classes in religious culture and moral education were made obligatory, and parents who wish their children to receive religious education outside school can obtain this under state supervision. However, in the Constitution of 1982, it is not stated who should provide this private religious education. The Law on the Establishment and Jurisdiction of the Presidency of Religious Affairs merely states in article 3 where this state-supervised religious education may take place.[49]

Perhaps the most important aspect of this article is that it only applies to Muslims. Turkish law makes no provision for the religious education of children whose parents belong to other faiths.[50] The wording of article 12 of the State Education Act appears to be a contradiction in terms as it states: "secularism shall be the basis of Turkish national education. Religious culture and ethics shall be among the compulsory subjects taught in primary and upper secondary schools, and in schools of these levels."[51]

It is the opinion of many politicians and legal experts that the State Education Act and the Constitution stipulate that religious education in schools is compulsory for Muslim children.[52] For instance, Ömer Çelik, who was Education Minister from 2011 to 2013, has reiterated many times that classes in Religious Culture and Ethics are compulsory.[53]

However, Kerem Altıparmak, who is a lawyer and an academic, does not agree. He puts forward the view that nothing in the Constitution says everyone has to attend classes in religious education. His interpretation of article 24, paragraph 4 is as follows: "It is compulsory for religious classes to be on the curriculum of schools at the primary and high school levels. The State is under an obligation to provide all students with this class as long as a student's parents do not object."[54] Altıparmak asserts that if the article is read in this way, it complies with article 13 of the Constitution, in that any limitations of fundamental rights and freedoms cannot violate the letter and spirit of the Constitution, or breach democratic society and the Republic of Turkey with its secular essence, or the principle of proportionality. Any limitations introduced should not affect fundamental rights. Altıparmak argues that religious education violates a fundamental right, the freedom of thought, conscience and religion. Since the Constitution does not stipulate that, all students have to attend religious education classes, to suggest there is such an obligation would contravene article 13 of the Constitution.[55]

In practice, despite these differing opinions, religious education has become a compulsory lesson for Muslim children. Although non-Muslims (Christians and Jews) were granted exemption by a regulation in 1990, as referred to above, article 24 of the Constitution does not mention exemption. Of course, for a person to have to reveal the fact they are Jewish or Christian in order to apply for exemption contravenes both article 24 of the Constitution and article 9 of the ECHR, which bans individuals being coerced into disclosing their faith.[56] The introduction of such an exemption increases the conjecture that the title 'religious culture and ethics' lessons is an effort to conceal the reality that the course teaches the Sunni interpretation of Islam.[57]

Although Jews and Christians have been granted certain freedoms in religious education (these are in any case guaranteed by the Treaty of Lausanne), the regulation of 1990 does not recognise the rights of those who are of other faiths or who are agnostic or atheist.[58] It is consequently apparent that Turkey is not meeting its obligations under international human rights law. As the EU Progress Report on Turkey in 2019 emphasised,

> [a] comprehensive legal framework in line with European standards needs to be put in place, and appropriate attention must be paid to implementing the ECtHR judgments on compulsory religion and ethics classes.[59]

As detailed above, following the *Zengin* judgment, the Alevi workshops were organised by the Turkish authorities. At the 18th National Council of Education held in November 2010, the issue of religious education was debated, and its significance as part of Turkish values was stressed. There was also agreement at the conference on the need to embrace a pluralist outlook.[60] The decision was also taken to provide optional religious classes (Koran -*Kuran-ı Kerim*-, Life of Prophet Muhammad -*Hz. Muhammed'in Hayatı*-, and Basic Religious Knowledge -*Temel Dini Bilgiler*) in order to assist parents who desired their children to be made aware of the ethical values mentioned in article 24 of the Constitution.[61]

Resolutions passed at the conference have subsequently been endorsed by academics involved in this debate. They have stated that these resolutions complied with the *Zengin* judgment as regards the content of religious education classes. But some scholars also criticised the resolutions.[62]

Some changes were also introduced after this conference, with article 9 of the Primary Education and Teaching Law and article 25 of Law no. 1739 (State Education Act) being amended thus:

> Optional courses shall be established in secondary and *İmam Hatip* secondary schools to support high school education according to the talents, development and preference of students. In secondary schools and high schools, the Koran and the life of our Prophet Muhammad shall be taught as an optional class on request. Other optional courses to be taught in these schools along with the curriculum alternatives yet to be established in *İmam Hatip* secondary and other secondary schools shall be determined by the Ministry.[63]

The above changes will do nothing to resolve the ongoing problem of the content of religious education as pointed out by the ECtHR, since the main subject taught remains the Sunni version of Islam. Of 504 hours of classes in 9 years, only 21 hours are allocated to explaining other beliefs such as the Alevi faith, Judaism, Christianity or Eastern religions.[64] In fact, it is obvious that an optional class has been introduced in order to provide instruction in the majority religion when requested by parents, whereas a compulsory class has to cover more than just one religion.[65]

However, it has been possible to observe noticeable changes in the approach of domestic courts since the *Zengin and Yalçın* judgments. For instance, the Council of State handed down a similar judgment in 2007.[66] It issued the following remark concerning students being compelled to memorise prayers and verses of the Koran:

> It is apparent that although the name of the education given in primary and secondary schools is called Religious Culture and Ethics, its content is not

acceptable as such. Indeed, in accordance with the findings made by the European Court of Human Rights with regard to the curriculum concerning teaching and considered sufficient for our judgment, the teaching of Religious Culture and Ethics in our country is not being carried out in an objective and rational understanding.[67]

The Council of State emphasised that religion classes should only be supplied if requested, remarking that to have compulsory Religious Culture and Ethics classes would constitute a violation of law in the event of there being no request for it.[68]

Similar judgments were handed down in 2008 and 2009.[69] Courts of First Instance have also made judgments along the same lines.[70] However, some Courts of First Instance have handed down judgments that totally contradict the Council of State judgment that is in accord with article 24 of the Constitution.[71] In 2009 the Ankara Administrative Court issued a judgment to the effect that religious education classes were non-denominational.[72]

A lower court judgment in 2010[73] was passed to the Council of State, where it was ratified by means of an expert report. It stressed that the lesson in question had been transformed into a Religious Culture and Ethics class, adding:

> It is not disputed that following the verdict in question that the new curriculum of the Religious Culture and Ethics lessons did not have the character of religious education, that its content should be accepted as religious culture and ethics teaching and that after the change in curriculum the applicant made an application....Hence it has been concluded that following changes in the curriculum religious culture and ethics education in our country is being provided in a pluralistic, objective and rational manner. As will be understood from the above at the time the applicant made application on 18 November 2008 the curriculum being implemented was not religious education, whereas the current Religious Culture and Ethics lessons now provided complies with article 24 of the Constitution and as such is compulsory.

Judgments handed down in 2011 and 2012 consolidated this judgment, and demands for a review of judgments have continued to fall on deaf ears in spite of the fact that the *Zengin and Yalçın* judgments present Turkey with clear human rights obligation.[74]

The judgments of the Council of State are clearly problematic. Most important of all, measures the Turkish Government took following the *Zengin* judgment in particular were not seen as sufficient by the Committee of Ministers. In spite of this, the Council of State considers the changes it made to be sufficient; therefore, it is not in agreement with the Committee of Ministers. The question at issue is not just a matter of educational content, but also affects the question of a child's right to freedom of religion and conscience. This right is linked to parents' right to make decisions concerning a child's education. Hence, the Council of State merits criticism for ignoring international conventions. Moreover, it is not in accordance with law to use an expert report as the basis of a judgment without the support of other justifications.[75]

Consequently, the Council of State judgment in question is clearly contrary to international human rights norms. At this juncture, it would be timely to remind ourselves that paragraph 5 of article 90 of the Constitution stresses the superiority of international norms to domestic provisions as regards human rights.[76] The above-mentioned paragraph of the Constitution states:

> International agreements duly put into effect carry the force of law. No appeal to the Constitutional Court shall be made with regard to these agreements, on the grounds that they are unconstitutional. *In the case of a conflict between international agreements in the area of fundamental rights and freedoms duly put into effect and the domestic laws due to differences in provisions on the same matter, the provisions of international agreements shall prevail.* (Italics added)

As highlighted above, once an international document is ratified and is published in the official gazette, the agreement becomes law and is superior to domestic law. This also implies that Turkey has positive responsibilities to guarantee the rights and freedoms contained in international documents which it has signed.[77] Hence, it is apparent that in spite of paragraph 5 of article 90 of the Turkish Constitution, domestic law and court judgments in Turkey conflict with international law.

4.4 Conclusion

The ECtHR has stated plainly in the *Zengin and Yalçın* judgments that religious education in Turkey does not meet the required standard and is not 'objective, pluralist and critical'. It has highlighted the fact that compulsory denominational (particularly Sunni) religious instruction is permitted, on the condition that it is possible for those who do not wish to attend such classes to apply for exemption.

Following the *Zengin and Yalçın* judgments, the Turkish authorities have endeavoured to transform compulsory religious education into cultural education, instead of putting an end to it. In addition to that, since 2012, optional classes on the Koran, Life of Prophet Muhammad and Basic Religious Knowledge have been added to the curriculum. However, these steps have not addressed the main issue, which is the question of the content of compulsory Religious Culture and Ethics lessons.

Moreover, no measures have been taken to address requests that classes be optional. The Council of State's stance is contrary to the ECtHR judgment and other international norms, constituting a serious obstacle to the inception of optional classes. It is obvious that compulsory religious education based on the teaching of a single religion contradicts the principle of a secular system. In fact, ever since Turkey was founded, the issue of religion has been controversial, and the place of religious education in a secular society and whether it should be provided by the State is yet to be conclusively decided. This situation also means children and parents suffer violations of the freedom of thought, religion and conscience.

Turkey, as a country that wishes to join the EU, has an obligation to comply with international norms. Making Religious Culture and Ethics classes optional would ensure compliance with international standards and also with the Turkish Constitution. Reform along these lines would also place Turkey in accord with other European countries, where there are optional classes or the right to exemption. Such a step would thus bring Turkey into line with current practice in Europe.

Notes

1. See A. Şaşmaz, B. Aydagül, I. Tüzün, İ. Aktaşlı, 'Türkiye'de Din ve Eğitim – Son Dönemdeki Gelişmeler ve Değişim Süreci', *Eğitim Reformu Girişimi* (2011), p. 22; Ensar Vakfı, 'Yeni Anayasa Taslağı ve Türkiye'de Din Eğitimi Meselesi Hakkında Ensar Vakfı'nin Görüşü', 1: 2 *Dem Dergisi* (2007), p. 52; R. Kaymakcan, 'Türkiye'de Din Eğitimi Politikaları Üzerine

Düşünceler', 10: 27 *EKEV Akademi Dergisi* (2006), p. 25; R. Kaymakcan, 'Yeni Ortaöğretim Din Kültürü ve Ahlak Bilgisi Öğretim Programı İnceleme ve Değerlendirme Raporu', *Eğitim Reformu Girişimi* (2007), pp. 10–15. Also see Ö. H. Çınar, 'Compulsory Religious Education in Turkey', 8 *Religion and Human Rights* (2013), pp. 223–241.
2. *Leirvåg and ors v. Norway*, 3 November 2004, No. CCPR/C/82/D/1155/2003.
3. Ibid., para. 14.7.
4. Ibid., para. 16.
5. For example, HRC, 25 April 2005, CCPR/CO/83/GRC (Concluding Observation: Greece).
6. HRC, General Comment no. 22, 'The Right to Freedom of Thought, Conscience and Religion', UN Doc. CCPR/C/21/Rev.1/Add.4, 30 July 1993, para. 6.
7. The Parliamentary Assembly of the Council of Europe, 4 October 2005, Recommendation no. 1720 (2005), paras. 14.1, 14.2.
8. Şaşmaz, Aydagül, Tüzün and Aktaşlı, *supra note* 1, p. 13.
9. *Angelini v. Sweden*, No. 10491/83, 51 DR 41 at 48 (1986); *Saniewski v. Poland*, 26 June 2001, No. 40319/98; *Folgerø and others v. Norway*, 29 June 2007, No. 15472/02.
10. *Grzelak v. Poland*, 15 June 2010, No. 7710/02.
11. Ibid., para. 100.
12. Ibid., para. 101.
13. *Hasan and Eylem Zengin v. Turkey*, 9 October 2007, No. 1448/04.
14. Ibid., para. 10.
15. Ibid., para. 13.
16. Ibid., paras. 36, 39.
17. Ibid., paras. 61–64, 67, 70 (references omitted).
18. Ibid., para. 76.
19. Ibid., para. 77.
20. Ibid., para. 79.
21. *Mansur Yalçın and others v. Turkey*, 26 September 2014, No. 21163/11.
22. For further information regarding the current state of execution of this case, see http://www.coe.int/t/dghl/monitoring/execution/Reports/pendingCases_en.asp?CaseTitleOrNumber=1448%2F04&StateCode=&SectionCode=, accessed 21 September 2020.
23. Article 46 states: "1. The High Contracting Parties undertake to abide by the final judgment of the Court in any case to which they are parties; 2. The final judgment of the Court shall be transmitted to the Committee of Ministers, which shall supervise its execution; 3. If the Committee of Ministers considers that the supervision of the execution of a final judgment is hindered by a problem of interpretation of the judgment, it may

refer the matter to the Court for a ruling on the question of interpretation. A referral decision shall require a majority vote of two thirds of the representatives entitled to sit on the committee; 4. If the Committee of Ministers considers that a High Contracting Party refuses to abide by a final judgment in a case to which it is a party, it may, after serving formal notice on that Party and by decision adopted by a majority vote of two thirds of the representatives entitled to sit on the committee, refer to the Court the question whether that Party has failed to fulfil its obligation under paragraph 1; 5. If the Court finds a violation of paragraph 1, it shall refer the case to the Committee of Ministers for consideration of the measures to be taken. If the Court finds no violation of paragraph 1, it shall refer the case to the Committee of Ministers, which shall close its examination of the case."

24. See *supra note 22*. Also see K. Altıparmak, *Hasan ve Eylem Zengin/Türkiye Kararının Uygulanması – İzleme Raporu*, http://aihmiz.org.tr/files/01_Hasan_ve_Eylem_Zengin_Rapor_TR.pdf, accessed 21 September 2020, p. 4.
25. Ministry of State *(Devlet Bakanlığı)*, *Alevi Çalıştayları Nihai Raporu* (Ankara: Devlet Bakanlığı, 2010), p. 192.
26. Norwegian Helsinki Committee, *2019 Report Pursuing Rights and Equality: Monitoring Report on the Right to Freedom of Religion or Belief in Turkey*, https://inancozgurlugugirisimi.org/wp-content/uploads/2019/08/Report_Turkey_ENG_web.pdf, accessed 21 September 2020, p. 37.
27. Norwegian Helsinki Committee, *supra note 26*, p. 38.
28. For further information about the history of religious education in Turkey including the era of Ottoman Empire, see M. Şanver, 'TBMM Tutanaklarına Göre Türkiye'de Din Eğitimi (1946–1957)', 1 *Sakarya Üniversitesi İlahiyat Fakültesi Dergisi* (1996), pp. 333–340; M. Ş. Aydın, *Cumhuriyet Döneminde Din Eğitimi Öğretmeni Yetiştirme ve İstihdamı (1923–1998)* (Ankara: IBAV, 2000), pp. 10–11; M. Öcal, *Osmanlı'dan Günümüze Türkiye'de Din Eğitimi Mukaddime Kitap* (Bursa: Düşünce Yayinevi, 2011); F. Alakuş and M. Bahçekapılı, *Din Eğitimi Açısından İngiltere ve Türkiye* (İstanbul: Ark, 2009), pp. 111–255; M. Sevim, 'Türkiye'de Cumhuriyet Dönemi Din Eğitimi ve Öğretimi Kronolojisi (1923'den Günümüze)', 1: 2 *Dem Dergisi* (2007), pp. 64–71.
29. Öcal, *supra note 28*, pp. 17–118; M. Öcal, 'Türkiye'de Din Eğitimi Tarihi Literatürü', 6–12 *Türkiye Araştırmaları Literatür Dergisi* (2008), pp. 399–402; Kaymakcan, 'Türkiye'de Din Eğitimi Politikaları Üzerine Düşünceler', *supra note 1*, p. 22.
30. Şanver, *supra note 28*, pp. 333–334; Öcal, *supra note 29*, pp. 402–406; M. A. Gökaçtı, *Türkiye'de Din Eğitimi ve İmam Hatipler* (İstanbul: İletişim, 2005), pp. 167–278.

31. Şanver, *supra note* 28, p. 335; T. Yürük, *Cumhuriyet Döneminde Türkiye'de Laiklik Çerçevesinde Din Eğitimi*, Master Dissertation (Adana: Çukurova University, 2005), pp. 86–87; Sevim, *supra note* 28, pp. 64–67.
32. Şanver, *supra note* 28, pp. 335–336; N. Kalaycı, *Cumhuriyet Döneminde İlköğretim* (İstanbul: Milli Eğitim Basımevi, 1988), p. 46.
33. For parliamentary debates, see *Türkiye Büyük Millet Meclisi Tutanak Dergisi*, Cilt III, pp. 428–445 and IV, pp. 420–594; Şanver, *supra note* 28, pp. 336–337 and Gökaçtı, *supra note* 30, pp. 168–172.
34. *Türkiye Büyük Millet Meclisi Tutanak Dergisi*, cilt III, p. 445. For further information, see Şanver, *supra note* 28, p. 336 and Gökaçtı, *supra note* 30, p. 171.
35. Şanver, *supra note* 28, p. 346.
36. The village institutes were operated between 1940 and 1954 to train teachers for only village schools.
37. Şanver, *supra note* 28, p. 338; *Milli Eğitim Bakanlığı Tebliğler Dergisi*, 7 February 1949, no. 524, p. 153; Sevim, *supra note* 28, pp. 64–71.
38. *Milli Eğitim Bakanlığı Tebliğler Dergisi*, 17 September 1956, no. 921; Sevim, *supra note* 28, p. 68; Şanver, *supra note* 28, p. 346.
39. Yürük, *supra note* 31, pp. 94–95.
40. V. Öztürk, *Din Eğitimi ve Siyaset*, PhD Thesis (İzmir: Dokuz Eylül University, 1997), pp. 96–119; Yürük, *supra note* 31, p. 96.
41. H. Ayhan, 'Cumhuriyet Dönemi Din Eğitimine Genel Bir Bakış', *A.Ü.İ.F. Dergisi Special Issue* (2009), p. 253; Yürük, *supra note* 31, p. 97.
42. National Security Council (1981), p. 181, cited in R. Kaymakcan, 'Religious Education Culture in Modern Turkey', in M. de Souza, G. Durka, K. Engebretson and R. Jackson (eds.), *International Handbook of the Religious, Moral and Spiritual Dimensions in Education* (The Netherlands: Springer, 2008), p. 450.
43. The Supreme Council for Education's Decision, no. 1, 9 July 1990 in *Milli Eğitim Bakanlığı Tebliğler Dergisi*, no. 2317, 23 July 1990.
44. Aydın, *supra note* 28, p. 124; Yürük, *supra note* 31, p. 98.
45. Board of Education and Discipline's decision, no. 373, 19 September 2000 in *Milli Eğitim Bakanlığı Tebliğler Dergisi*, no. 2571, volume 63, October 2000.
46. Board of Education and Discipline's decision, no. 16, 31 May 2005.
47. B. Kuzu, 'Türkiye'de Anayasal Planda ve Uygulamada İnsan Hak ve Hürriyetlerine Genel Bir Bakış', *İnsan Hakları* (1995), p. 228; H. S. Demir, *Türkiye'de Din ve Vicdan Özgürlüğü* (Ankara: Adalet, 2011), p. 153.
48. *Campbell and Cosans v. United Kingdom*, 25 February 1982, Nos. 7511/76, 7743/76, para. 33.
49. Article 3 states: "Apart from the compulsory Religious Culture and Ethics classes taught in primary and secondary institutions, for those who wish to learn the Koran and its meaning, to become one who has memorised the

Koran and receive religious education having completed primary education, Koran courses shall be opened by the Presidency of Religious Affairs. The religious education and instruction on these courses shall be subject to the wish of the individual and, in the case of minors, to the request of their legal representatives. Additionally, summer Koran courses shall be opened for those who have completed the fifth year of primary school under the supervision of the Ministry of National Education" (see the Law on the Establishment and Jurisdiction of the Presidency of Religious Affairs, Law no. 633, adopted on 22 June 1965, Official gazette dated 2 July 1965 (No. 12038)). For education in Koran courses, see K. Gözler, *1982 Anayasasına Göre Din Eğitimi ve Öğretimi*, http://www.anayasa.gen.tr/din-egitimi.htm, accessed 21 September 2020.
50. Demir, *supra note* 47, p. 154.
51. State Education Act, Law no. 1739, adopted 14 June 1973, Official gazette dated 24 June 1973 (No. 14574).
52. Gözler, *supra note* 49; Demir, *supra note* 47, pp. 153–154; Ensar Vakfı, *supra note* 1, p. 53.
53. 'Zorunlu Din Dersi Anayasal Bir Gereklilik', *CNN Turk*, 22 December 2012, http://www.cnnturk.com/2012/Türkiye/12/22/zorunlu.din.dersi.anayasal.gereklilik/689702.0/index.html, accessed 21 September 2020.
54. K. Altıparmak, 'Zorunlu Din Dersi Gerçekten Zorunlu mu?', *Radikal2*, 13 February 2005.
55. Ibid.
56. For example, *Buscarini and others* v. *San Marino*, 18 February 1999, No. 24645/94; *Sinan Işık* v. *Turkey*, 2 February 2010, No. 21924/05.
57. Demir, *supra note* 47, p. 156; Gözler, *supra note* 49; Altıparmak, *supra note* 24, p. 10; B. Özenç, *Avrupa İnsan Hakları Sözleşmesi ve İnanç Özgürlüğü* (İstanbul: Kitap Yayınevi, 2006), p. 126.
58. On 24 July 1923, the Treaty of Lausanne was signed by the British Empire, France, Italy, Japan, Greece, Romania and the 'Serbo-Croat-Slovene' State on one side and Turkey on the other.
59. European Commission, *Turkey 2019 Progress Report*, SWD (2019) 220 final, pp. 31–32.
60. Minister of National Education *(Milli Eğitim Bakanlığı)*, 18th National Council of Education's decisions, http://www.meb.gov.tr/duyurular/duyurular2010/ttkb/18Sura_kararlari_tamami.pdf, accessed 21 September 2020, para. 39.
61. Ibid., para. 43.
62. See Kaymakcan, 'Türkiye'de Din Eğitimi Politikaları Üzerine Düşünceler', *supra note* 1, pp. 28–30. Also see H. Ayhan, *Türkiye'de Din Eğitimi*

(İstanbul: M.Ü. İFAV Yayınları, 1999); Eğitim Reform Girişimi, *Türkiye'de Din ve Eğitimi: Değişim İhtiyacı* (İstanbul: Sabancı Üniversitesi Eğitim Reform Girişimi, 2005).
63. Amended Primary Education and Teaching Law, no. 6287, 30 March 2012, Official gazette dated 11 April 2012 (No. 28261).
64. B. Özenç, 'AİHM ve Danıştay Kararlarının Ardından Zorunlu Din Dersleri Sorunu', LXVI–2 *İstanbul Üniversitesi Hukuk Fakültesi Mecmuası* (2008), p. 224. Also see Norwegian Helsinki Committee, *supra note* 26, p. 38.
65. Altıparmak, *supra note* 24, p. 6.
66. The Council of State (8. Chamber), 28 December 2007, E. 2006/4107, K. 2007/7481.
67. Ibid., p. 9.
68. Demir, *supra note* 47, p. 159.
69. The Council of State (8. Chamber), 29 February 2008, E. 2007/679, K. 2008/1461; The Council of State (8. Chamber), 15 May 2009, E. 2007/8365, K. 2009/3238.
70. For example, Sakarya 2. Administrative Court, 29 June 2010, E. 2009/877, K. 2010/546; Sivas Administrative Court, 22 July 2010, E. 2009/1259, K. 2010/870; İstanbul 1. Administrative Court, 7 October 2010, E. 2010/136, K. 2010/1408; Ankara 1. Administrative Court, 29 April 2011, E. 2010/1042, K. 2011/624.
71. Ankara 14. Administrative Court, 15 December 2010, E. 2008/1394, K. 2010/1783.
72. Ankara 10. Administrative Court, 1 October 2009, E. 2005/2703, K. 2009/1804.
73. The Council of State (8. Chamber), 13 July 2010, E. 2009/10610, K. 2010/2413.
74. The Council of State (8. Chamber), 29 November 2011, E. 2011/5904, K. 2011/6141; The Council of State (8. Chamber), 23 May 2012, E. 2012/2599, K. 2012/3401; The Council of State (8. Chamber), 8 June 2012, E. 2010/8381, K. 2012/4640.
75. See Altıparmak, *supra note* 24, p. 15.
76. See, for example, A. Gündüz, *Milletlerarası Hukuk Temel Belgeler – Örnek Kararlar* (İstanbul: Beta Basım, 4th Edition, 2000); E. Memiş, 'İnsan Hakları Avrupa Standardı ve İç Hukuk Etkileşimi Analizleri', 17 *Anayasa Yargısı* (2000), pp. 130–173.
77. Articles 15(1) and 16 of the 1982 Constitution. For further information on positive obligations, also see J-F. Akandji-Kombe, *Positive Obligations under the European Convention on Human Rights: A guide to the implementation of the European Convention on Human Rights* (Strasbourg: Council of Europe, 2007).

CHAPTER 5

Recognition of Faith Groups and the Opening of Places of Worship

Abstract This chapter firstly addresses the international standards on the issue of places of worship, including the right to have a legal personality, the right to open a place of worship, the right to teach one's religion and belief, and the right to appoint religious officials. Secondly, it examines whether Turkey has met these standards. Hence, this chapter will explore the relevant provisions in Turkish law and how Turkish courts interpret both domestic and international laws.

Keywords Faith groups • Places of worship • Legal personality • Religious officials/leaders • Turkey • International and domestic/national law • *forum externum*

5.1 Introduction

According to article 10 of the Constitution of the Republic of Turkey, everyone is equal before the law without distinction as to language, race, colour, gender, political opinion, philosophical belief, religion and sect or any such grounds. The State is consequently obliged to take the necessary steps to ensure that this equality is implemented. This concept of equality includes benefiting from public services. If access to religious services is also a kind of public service, then the State must treat all manner of religion equally. However, it is necessary to ask whether minorities enjoy equality in a country where Sunni Islam is the dominant understanding.

In this chapter in which the Treaty of Lausanne will be closely examined, despite it not being clear who was intended by the term 'non-Muslim minority', in practice the Rum (Greek), Armenian and Jewish have been accepted as minorities and their rights safeguarded, while other religious groups—Protestants, Bahá'ís, Jehovah's Witnesses and Yezidis—have unfortunately not been recognised as religious minorities. So, what will happen to the rights of these minorities? In practice, does the Treaty of Lausanne really have force?

Apart from these minorities, Turkey's largest religious/faith minority community, the Alevis, has expressed their desire to manifest their beliefs freely and equally on several platforms. However, as mentioned in other chapters, there is the reality of the Presidency of Religious Affairs (*Diyanet İşleri Başkanlığı*—*Diyanet*) in Turkey, and the question as to whether it promotes Sunni Islam will also be examined in this chapter. For, as mentioned in previous chapters, the *Diyanet* states there is no distinction between Alevis and Sunnis, that Alevis are a sect within the religion of Islam and does not recognise a separate Alevi belief. Hence, despite Alevi opposition, it persists in building mosques in Alevi villages. While there are more than 80,000 mosques under the auspices of the *Diyanet*, the cemevi, the places of worship of Alevis, are not recognised.[1] In Turkey, apart from the Alevis, the Syrian Orthodox community is still awaiting permission to open its own churches in İstanbul. While religious and faith groups face such difficulties, there has also been a rise in hate crimes. Hence, the 2019 European Union (EU) Progress Report states: "Hate speech and threats directed against minorities remain a serious problem. This includes hate speech in the media targeting national, ethnic and religious groups."[2]

However, while a country endeavouring to join the EU has obligations to comply with EU standards, in order to examine whether Turkey has met these standards, reference will be made both to the safeguards for religious minorities in EU member countries and to the provisions in this regard in international law. This will be followed by an examination of the relevant provisions in Turkish law and how Turkish courts interpret both domestic and international laws.

5.2 International Law Standards

When it is considered that Turkey is a member of both the UN and the Council of Europe, it is very important to understand its obligations arising from international law, particularly as since 2005 it has been endeavouring to join the EU.

The manifestation of religion and belief in the public sphere includes the right to open places of worship. Krishnaswami indicates that States set up obstacles to prevent religious minorities from exercising their rights by the use of 'unreasonable regulations'—for instance, by extending the process of obtaining permission for places of worship or schools or by making the criteria more difficult to meet, going as far as intimidation.[3]

Article 18 of the International Covenant on Civil and Political Rights (ICCPR) states that everyone has the right: "either individually or in community with others and in public or private, to manifest his religion or belief in worship, observance, practice and teaching". Paragraph 3 of the same article states: "Freedom to manifest one's religion or beliefs may be subject only to such limitations as are prescribed by law and are necessary to protect public safety, order, health, or morals or the fundamental rights and freedoms of others." This article expresses the *forum externum* dimension of the freedom of religion and belief, over which States have the right of discretion. However, when imposing limitations, the criteria are clearly set forth in paragraph 3.

Regarding article 18, the Human Rights Committee (HRC) made the following General Comment at its 22nd session:

> The freedom to manifest religion or belief in worship, observance, practice and teaching encompasses a broad range of acts. The concept of worship extends to ritual and ceremonial acts giving direct expression to belief, as well as various practices integral to such acts, including the building of places of worship, the use of ritual formulae and objects, the display of symbols, and the observance of holidays and days of rest. The observance and practice of religion or belief may include not only ceremonial acts but also such customs as the observance of dietary regulations, the wearing of distinctive clothing or head coverings, participation in rituals associated with certain stages of life, and the use of a particular language customarily spoken by a group. In addition, the practice and teaching of religion or belief includes acts integral to the conduct by religious groups of their basic affairs, such as the freedom to choose their religious leaders, priests and teachers, the freedom to establish seminaries or religious schools and the freedom to prepare and distribute religious texts or publications.[4]

Article 9 of the European Convention on Human Rights (ECHR) is almost identical in wording to paragraphs 1 and 3 of article 18 of the ICCPR. Paragraph 1 of article 18 of the ICCPR sets out the general parameters of the freedom of thought, conscience and religion, while paragraph 3 mentions the situations in which this right may be limited, the margin of appreciation. A three-stage test is used by the European Court of Human Rights (ECtHR) with regard to the restricting of this freedom:

(a) Any intervention by the authorities must be in accordance with law, including statutes, decree laws, codes, regulations and court judgments.[5] The legislation cited must be precise and contain safeguards to prevent the authorities taking arbitrary measures.[6] That is, the provisions should offer protection by precluding arbitrary intervention through foreseeability and accessibility safeguards.[7]

(b) Any justification for intervention should include one of the legitimate aims mentioned in article 9(2), public safety, public order, health or morals, or be in order to protect the rights and freedoms of others.

The Court asks this question at the second stage. As the State has an obligation to explain the reason for the interference, and because there are broad grounds to justify any interference—one that is often cited is public safety—a State generally sets out an acceptable reason for its intervention. Although applicants often claim that the reason put forward by the State is not the actual reason for the interference in question, the Court has in general not acceded to such claims. In fact, the Court has as a rule not examined in detail the justifications put forward by the State as the grounds for its actions. The Court has tended to merge the reasons cited, for instance, the protection of health and morals and the protection of the rights and freedoms of others, into a single aim.[8] Consequently, the Court has been very reluctant to reject the reasons cited by States and has in general accepted that the intervention in question was made for the purpose stated. Even in cases where the applicant has disputed the reasons given, this has been the attitude of the Court.[9]

(c) It 'must be necessary in a democratic society'. This implies that there must 'be a pressing social need',[10] for any intervention and that it must 'be proportionate to the legitimate aim pursued'.[11] As regards a 'democratic society', this means a society that is based on the principles of pluralism, tolerance and open-mindedness.[12] It is not enough for a State to claim 'some' justification for the measures it has taken, as any interference must be 'necessary'. When it comes to the meaning of 'necessary', in *Handyside v. the UK*, the Court remarked that it is not synonymous with "indispensable"…neither has it the flexibility of such expressions as "admissible", "ordinary", "useful", "reasonable" or "desirable".[13]

As regards the matter of pressing social need, States have a margin of appreciation.[14] On account of the complexity and sensitivity of some cases, national authorities may be in a position to make a better consideration of a case in their own circumstances and make a decision as to what steps need to be taken.[15] This margin of appreciation does, of course, vary according to circumstances, the issue being addressed and its background.[16]

While State parties have a margin of appreciation, they also have obligations as regards this right. In short, States must meet their positive and negative obligations arising from the Convention at all times while the margin of appreciation is being utilised. These obligations are spelled out in article 1 of the Convention. This article states that High Contracting Parties must ensure everyone in their jurisdiction enjoys the rights and freedoms defined in the Convention. It is therefore the negative obligation of States to protect the exercise of this freedom and ensure there is no arbitrary interference. Hence, the main aim of article 9 is to ensure individuals are safeguarded against arbitrary interference by public authorities.

States also have positive obligations to ensure that legal entities act respectfully towards each other.[17] However, the Court has not defined the meaning of the concept 'respect' in this context. Therefore, the meaning of respect varies depending on the situation. Although there is a definition of what respect necessitates according to circumstances, States have a very broad margin of appreciation. The State is obliged to ensure that there is a fair balance between the general interests of the individual and those of society.[18] The scope of positive obligations includes the 'obligation to take measures' and 'obligation to be effective'. Such obligations are as follows: to make legal provisions for the issue in question and to supervise and undertake a fair and unbiased investigation. States have the responsibility to achieve effective outcomes as regards these measures.[19]

5.2.1 European Court of Human Rights' Case Law

As emphasised in the jurisprudence of the ECtHR, the freedom of religion is not just an individual right, but also has a social dimension. Article 9 of the ECHR grants States a margin of appreciation on the question of places of worship. For instance, States have a margin of appreciation as regards planning law or site selection. However, this does not include the power to question the religious ceremonies of a religious community.[20]

Article 9 of the Convention safeguards the right to open and maintain buildings for the purpose of religious worship. Thus, in some circumstances, the use of religious buildings may impact on members of religious groups exercising the right to manifest religious belief.[21]

Furthermore, the Court has in a judgment agreed that in the event of a religious community being denied a place of worship, its right to manifest its religion is violated.[22] Even if some religious meetings are permitted or merely tolerated by the domestic authorities, there may still be a risk of interference.[23]

The terms of article 9 do not give a religious community the right to demand from the authorities a place of worship.[24] Moreover, State toleration for the continued use of a State-owned building for religious ceremonies for several years does not impose a positive obligation on those authorities.[25] However, if a religious community owns a building and cannot obtain a long-term lease on the land on which it stands in order to construct a new place of worship to meet the community's needs, there may be issues under article 9.[26]

Article 9 also does not grant a religious community the right to the repossession of a building of worship that was seized by the State a long time ago (in the 1930s, in the case in question) by the authorities of the time.[27] Additionally, article 9 does not prevent the domestic authorities from ordering that two different religious communities should use a place of worship alternately, where specific historical circumstances exist.[28]

Furthermore, the Convention does not impose any obligation on the State to grant special status to places of worship. However, if a State does offer privileged status to places of worship—exceeding its obligations under the Convention—it cannot do this in a discriminatory way contrary to article 14 to benefit particular religious groups.[29]

In general, States enjoy a broad margin of appreciation as regards spatial development, a complex and difficult issue, when it comes to urban-planning policy. This is due to the fact that planning legislation is seen as necessary in modern society in order to prevent uncontrolled development.[30] Hence, urban-planning regulations are deemed to be in harmony with the legitimate purpose of safeguarding public order as enshrined in article 9(2) of the Convention.[31] However, the Court has powers of review, and it must satisfy itself that the necessary balance has been struck in line with the applicants' right to the freedom to manifest their religion.[32] Furthermore, in the event that national authorities have considered freedom of religion when evaluating planning, it is not possible for a religious organisation to use the rights in article 9 to get around planning legislation. It is important that the authorities have regard to the specific needs of small religious communities when attempting to strike a balance.[33]

To summarise, while the Court defines broadly the right to manifest religion and belief and in what circumstances limitations may be placed on this right, a more detailed examination of sample cases will provide greater understanding. In the cases mentioned below, the Court found a violation of article 9.

In *Manoussakis and others v. Greece*, the Court examined the prosecution of Jehovah's Witnesses for worshipping at a place without permission. The Court criticised the role given to the Orthodox Church in defining a place of worship in Greece and the restrictions imposed on religious minorities. Consequently, the Court found that article 9 had been violated since the Greek legislation in question, on which the conviction of the applicants was based, placed limitations on the activities of religious communities outside the Greek Orthodox Church and was not proportionate as regards a legitimate aim and was not necessary in a democratic society. The State does not have the discretion to restrict the right to freedom of religion or to judge the legitimacy or otherwise of religious beliefs or the way such beliefs are manifested.[34]

However, from this judgment, the conclusion should not be drawn that religious communities have unlimited rights as regards opening a place of worship. In the case of *Tanyar and Küçükergin v. Turkey*, where the applicants were prohibited from using an apartment in a building for worship without obtaining permission from other residents, the Court did not find a violation of article 9. The protection of the rights of others living in the building was defined as a legitimate aim.[35]

Another recent judgment by the Court concerning Turkey is the case of *Cumhuriyetçi Eğitim ve Kültür Merkezi Vakfı v. Turkey*. The applicant organisation, the Cumhuriyetçi Eğitim ve Kültür Merkezi Vakfı, or CEM Vakfı (the Foundation for Republican Education and Culture), is a foundation that was established in accordance with Turkish law in 1995. The application was based on a provision in Turkish law that makes it possible for places of worship to be exempt from paying electricity bills and the Turkish authorities' refusal to allow the applicant foundation to enjoy this privilege. The Court found in a judgment of 2 December 2014 that article

14 combined with article 9 had been violated on the grounds that the Turkish regulation on the exemption for places of worship for electricity bills was legal discrimination on a religious basis.[36] Consequently, the ECtHR found that the way the *CEM Vakfi* had been treated was neither objective nor acceptable. However, despite this judgment in 2014, Turkey has still not taken the step of recognising cemevi as places of worship as required by the judgment.[37]

Apart from the rights of religious groups regarding places of worship, the Court has also addressed the issue of prosecutions on account of individuals' beliefs. For instance, in the case of *Masaev v. Moldova*, the applicants claimed that article 9 had been violated on account of their beliefs, as Muslims, not being recognised by the authorities and that they had been fined for worshipping together. The Court found the fine imposed by the State on members of an unrecognised religion to be disproportionate; otherwise, the State would have the right to ostracise minority faiths and to decide on what individuals may or may not believe. The Court said this would be unacceptable and found there had been a violation of article 9.[38]

In the case of *Dimitrova v. Bulgaria*, the applicant was asked to go to the local police station where she was questioned about her religious beliefs. Her home was subsequently searched and books and recordings were seized, after which the police ordered the applicant to stop hosting meetings of the evangelical group of which she was a member. The Court found that there was no reason in law for the interference and that the measures had been taken in blatant breach of domestic law, as no criminal investigation had been initiated.[39] This judgment is significant, as it demonstrates that States may not restrict this freedom in an unlimited manner.

The Court has also handed down important judgments on the question of the existence and management of religious communities. The judgments regarding Muslim minorities in Greece and Bulgaria in particular are important in this regard. In the case of *Serif v. Greece*, Serif was a theological graduate who was elected as Mufti (religious official) in a region of Greece.[40] After the previous Mufti had died, an interim Mufti had been appointed by the State. Five years later, Muslim MPs asked for an election to decide who would take up the post of Mufti and Serif was elected. He thus began to operate as a Mufti, dressed in the traditional clothes warranted by the post. He was charged "for having usurped the functions of a minister of a known religion and for having publicly worn the dress of such a minister without having the right to do so".[41] He was fined for this offence. The applicant referred to article 11 of the Treaty of Peace of Athens (17 March 1913), a Turkish-Greek treaty that set out that Muslims would elect their Muftis themselves. However, the State argued that since the duties of Muftis included judicial tasks, and judges were not elected by the people, this meant Muslims too did not have this right. The State argued that it had acted in order to prevent a possible split in the Muslim community, but this did not grant the Greek State the right to remove Mr Serif. "Although the Court recognises that it is possible that tension is created in situations where a religious or any other community becomes divided, it considers that this is one of the unavoidable consequences of pluralism. The role of the authorities in such circumstances is not to remove the cause of tension by eliminating pluralism, but to ensure that the competing groups tolerate each other."[42] Hence, as the interference was not considered to be "necessary in a democratic society…, for the protection of public order" under article 9(2) of the Convention, the Court found that there had been a violation of article 9.

In the case of *Hassan and Chaush v. Bulgaria*, Hasan was Chief Mufti of Bulgarian Muslims from 1992, and Chaush was a Muslim teacher who then became secretary of the Islamic Institute in Sofia.[43] Following democratisation, the previous Chief Mufti had been sacked after it was alleged that he had collaborated with the Communist authorities. However, in November 1994, the previous Chief Mufti organised a meeting, changed the regulations and restored himself to the position of Chief Mufti. The Offices of the Chief Mufti were then occupied by a group which seized all papers and assets. The Government refused to support the applicant, Hasan the Chief Mufti, as they had accepted the statute of November 1994, adding that it was not possible for there to be two Islamic associations. After talks with the Directorate of Religious Denominations, a reunification meeting took place in 1997 and the Government declared that the previous Chief Mufti did not have the right to represent Bulgarian Muslims in the intervening years. The applicants argued that the State had interfered with their right to organise their faith, whereas the Government claimed that they had not in any way prevented expressions of religious belief, for example, prayer and other kinds of worship.

In this judgment, the Court set down the fundamental principles on the question of the organisation of religious communities, imposing significant duties in this regard on Contracting States:

The Court recalls that religious communities traditionally and universally exist in the form of organised structures. They abide by rules which are often seen by followers as being of a divine origin. Religious ceremonies have their meaning and sacred value for the believers if they have been conducted by ministers empowered for that purpose in compliance with these rules. The personality of the religious ministers is undoubtedly of importance to every member of the community. Participation in the life of the community is thus a manifestation of one's religion, protected by article 9 of the Convention.

Where the organisation of the religious community is at issue, article 9 of the Convention must be interpreted in the light of article 11, which safeguards associative life against unjustified State interference. Seen in this perspective, the believers' right to freedom of religion encompasses the expectation that the community will be allowed to function peacefully, free from arbitrary State intervention. Indeed, the autonomous existence of religious communities is indispensable for pluralism in a democratic society and is thus an issue at the very heart of the protection which article 9 affords. It directly concerns not only the organisation of the community as such but also the effective enjoyment of the right to freedom of religion by all its active members. Were the organisational life of the community not protected by article 9 of the Convention, all other aspects of the individual's freedom of religion would become vulnerable.[44]

As a result, the Court found in this case that there had been a violation of article 9. For it concluded that the State's right to intervene did not include the condition of 'foreseeable law', as this ran the risk of the State authorities using their powers in an arbitrary way.

The Court in the case of *Bessarabia Metropolitan Church and others v. Moldova* examined the reasons why the authorities did not recognise this church, finding a violation of article 9. The Court stated:

[S]ince religious communities traditionally exist in the form of organised structures, article 9 must be interpreted in the light of article 11 of the Convention, which safeguards associative life against unjustified State interference. Seen in that perspective, the right of believers to freedom of religion, which includes the right to manifest one's religion in community with others, encompasses the expectation that believers will be allowed to associate freely, without arbitrary State intervention. Indeed, the autonomous existence of religious communities is indispensable for pluralism in a democratic society and is thus an issue at the very heart of the protection which article 9 affords...

In addition, one of the means of exercising the right to manifest one's religion, especially for a religious community, in its collective dimension, is the possibility of ensuring judicial protection of the community, its members and its assets, so that article 9 must be seen not only in the light of article 11, but also in the light of article 6.[45]

This ruling of the Court continued in further cases, including certain cases concerning the property rights of religious communities in Turkey.[46] The issue in question is that of religious communities' right to be a legal personality as enshrined in article 9 of the ECHR combined with article 11 of the ECHR. The Court underlines that a religious community has the right in accordance with article 9 to define its internal religious concepts and sects without the interference of secular authorities.[47]

To summarise, as can be seen in these judgments, no State has the right to define religious ceremonies or places of worship. States are, in particular, expected to observe the principle of impartiality. However, as in Turkey where, on account of the religious authorities (*Diyanet*) not defining the Alevis as a faith group, they still experience difficulties in worshiping in their own places of worship. This is a blatant example of Turkey's non-implementation of ECtHR judgments, an issue which will be examined in detail in the next chapter.

5.2.2 The EU and the Venice Commission

Apart from Court judgments, Turkey's responsibilities as a country that has been engaged in a process to become a member of the EU since 2005 should also be considered. Hence, the EU Progress Report of 2019 states that "[r]egarding minorities, full respect for and protection of language, religion, culture and fundamental rights in accordance with European standards have yet to be fully achieved".[48]

According to paragraph 1 of article 10 of the EU Charter of Fundamental Rights, everyone has the right to manifest their religious beliefs alone or in a group 'in worship, teaching, practice and observance'. However, unlike the ICCPR and ECHR, the circumstances when this right may be restricted are not mentioned. But this, of course, does not mean that the right cannot have limitations placed on it. In judgments of the International Court of Justice in 2018 was the following:

[I]t must be observed that the Charter uses the word 'religion' in a broad sense, covering both the *forum internum*, that is the fact of having a belief, and the *forum externum*, that is the manifestation of religious faith in public.[49]

The International Court of Justice also refers to the two dimensions of this freedom in its case law, demonstrating by the way it interprets this freedom that it is not different to the ECtHR.[50]

If mention is to be made of the rights of religious minorities, then it is necessary to refer to the Venice Commission. Hence, in the EU Progress Report of 2019, there is mention of the recommendations of the Venice Commission, saying that Turkey must continue its reform process on minority rights and enact legal provisions that allow non-Muslim communities to obtain legal personality status.[51]

The Venice Commission, also known by its official title of the European Commission for Democracy through Law, is a consultative body of the Council of Europe consists of independent experts. This commission makes certain recommendations regarding the legal status of religious communities in Turkey. Hence, the 'opinion' below was presented at the 82nd Session of the Venice Commission:

In view of the strict requirements established in the case-law of the European Court of Human Rights, the Venice Commission sees no reason which would justify not granting to religious communities as such the possibility to obtain legal personality. It therefore recommends that Turkey should introduce legislation that would make it possible for religious communities as such to acquire and maintain legal personality...In the meantime, until such a general reform may be adopted, the Venice Commission urges the Turkish authorities to interpret and apply the present legal system (the laws on foundations and associations) in such a way as to minimise the restrictions on the exercise of religious freedom of the non-Muslim religious communities. This calls for a liberal and flexible interpretation and application both of the two statutes and with regard to article 24 of the Constitution, article 101 of the Civil Code, and other potentially relevant rules...As regards the law on associations, there seems at present to be a problem with registering associations wholly or partly for religious purposes. There seems to be a lack of clarity in Turkish legislation, and administrative discretion tends to be exercised in a way not favourable to religious communities. This is shown by the example of Jehovah's Witnesses, who had to go to court to obtain the right to register an association to support their religion. The Venice

Commission therefore recommends that the Turkish authorities interpret and apply the present law on associations in such a way as to allow for religious communities as such to register as associations. As regards the law on foundations, there seem at present to be various problems with regard to the property ownership of the religious communities. The basic problem is that they cannot hold property themselves, but have to go through a foundation. This should be remedied. But as long as this is not done, then this makes it all the more important under the ECHR and other European standards that this is a fairly easily accessible system—making it easy to set up new foundations, or for old foundations to register new property and to exercise effective ownership control over the existing properties. In this regard it is particularly troubling that article 101 (4) of the Civil Code as interpreted by the authorities and the Turkish courts seem to prohibit the setting up of new foundations with the aim of supporting a specific religious community or specific activities of such a community. The Venice Commission cannot see any legitimate reason why it should not be possible to set up a foundation for the purposes of a specific religious community or for specific religious activities. The Commission therefore recommends that article 101 (4) of the Civil Code should not be interpreted and applied so as to prohibit the establishment or maintenance of foundations with the purpose of supporting religious communities or activities. In addition, all outstanding cases concerning the question of return of property seized by the authorities after 1974 should be dealt with and resolved in a manner compatible with the requirements of the ECHR.[52]

5.3　Turkey's Obligations

Despite these recommendations of the Venice Commission, at the time these lines were written, Turkey had still not taken serious steps in this field. Hence, the rights of religious minority groups in Turkey are a constant subject of debate, which in fact have their origins in the Ottoman Empire. For instance, in the Ottoman period there were many massacres carried out against the Alevis, in particular the slaughter of 40,000 Alevis by Sultan Selim the First (the Grim), which has gone down as a dark stain in history.[53]

After victory in the War of Independence and during the founding of the Republic, the Treaty of Lausanne was signed. This treaty, which was signed on 24 July 1923 by representatives of the Republic of Turkey, the British Empire, French Republic, Kingdom of Italy, Empire of Japan, Kingdom of Greece, Kingdom of Romania and the Kingdom of Serbs,

Croats and Slovenes (Yugoslavia), is worthy of mention. Articles 38–44 of this treaty envisage the protection of all legal and political rights of non-Muslim minorities. However, the Treaty does not make clear by non-Muslim who is meant. However, in practice, the Armenian Apostolic (Orthodox), Greek Orthodox and Jewish communities are the communities specified.[54] According to article 40, non-Muslims have the right to establish, run and control their own charitable and educational institutions. They may even freely use their own languages. Article 42(2) of the Treaty deals with the ability to establish religious institutions.

Although the rights of non-Muslims were safeguarded in the Treaty by these provisions, in practice there is no protection of the rights of other communities, such as the Latin Catholic, Syriac Chaldean and Bahá'í. Additionally, the situation of the Alevis, a group that interprets Islam in a different way and numbers up to 25 million people, is not very different.[55]

Even as these lines are being written, there is still serious repression of minority religious and faith groups in Turkey. Hence, bodies such as the Council of Europe, the Venice Commission and the European Union mention this oppression in their reports. The Chapter on Turkey in the 2020 Annual Report of the US Commission on International Religious Freedom summarises the current situation in the following way:

> [R]eligious freedom conditions in Turkey remained worrisome, with the perpetuation of restrictive and intrusive governmental policies on religious practice and a marked increase in incidents of vandalism and societal violence against religious minorities. As in previous years, the government continued to unduly interfere in the internal affairs of religious communities by preventing the election of board members for non-Muslim foundations and introducing new limitations on the long-delayed election of the Armenian Apostolic Church's patriarch. The Interior Ministry curtailed the candidacies of certain individuals in the latter election despite a May 2019 Constitutional Court ruling that prior acts of such state interference had violated religious freedom. Alevis, the country's largest religious minority community, remained unable to gain official recognition for their gathering houses (cemevleri) as places of worship or to exempt their children from compulsory religious classes, despite European Court of Human Rights rulings finding that these policies violated Alevis' rights. Religious minorities in Turkey expressed concerns that governmental rhetoric and policies contributed to an increasingly hostile environment and implicitly encouraged acts of societal aggression and violence. Government officials and poli-

ticians continued to propagate expressions of anti-Semitism and hate speech, and no progress was made during the year to repeal Turkey's blasphemy law…Many longstanding issues concerning religious sites, such as the inability of the Greek Orthodox community to train clergy at the Halki Seminary, remained unresolved. In several instances in 2019, Armenian, Assyrian, and Greek religious and cultural sites, including numerous cemeteries, faced severe damage or destruction—in some cases because of neglect, but also due to vandalism or state-endorsed construction projects—while Alevi holy sites in the province of Sivas faced similar threats after the government issued mining permits for the surrounding area.[56]

In response to this report, Turkey says it is not true and impartial. Furthermore, it claims that the report is a clear example of US neglect and bias in the anti-terror struggle. It has the view that religious minorities in Turkey live in peace with equal rights in law, as they have done for decades, and that their freedom of religion is safeguarded.[57]

In brief, the statements of religious and faith groups in Turkey and those of the Turkish authorities contradict each other. In this context, it will be useful to take a close look at the provisions in Turkish law regarding this question and the interpretation of courts in the country.

5.3.1 *Turkish Law*

Since in other chapters of this book provisions relating to the freedom of conscience and religion in the Turkish Constitution are examined, there will not be a detailed analysis here. If it is necessary to summarise, provisions regarding this freedom are to be found in articles 2, 10, 14, 24 and 174 of the Constitution.

In article 2 it is indicated that the Republic of Turkey is a secular state, which is important as the principle of secularism is, of course, essential for providing the conditions in which this freedom can be exercised to its fullest extent.[58]

Article 10 sets out the principle of equality, stating that everyone is equal, regardless of religion or sect. Hence, the Constitutional Court handed down a judgment to the effect that there could not be discrimination between Abrahamic religions and other religions, mentioning the importance of the principle of equality.[59]

As for article 24, it deals with the freedom of conscience and religion, indicating that everyone has the freedom of conscience, religious belief and conviction. It states that acts of worship, religious rites and ceremonies shall be conducted freely, as long as they do not violate the provisions of article 14. This article also stipulates that no one shall be compelled to worship, or to participate in religious rites and ceremonies, or to reveal religious beliefs and convictions, or be blamed or accused because of their religious beliefs and convictions.

This article refers to article 14, in that it pertains to the prohibition of exploiting or abusing fundamental rights and freedoms. Hence, in accordance with article 14, none of the rights and freedoms embodied in the Constitution shall be exercised in the form of activities aiming to violate the indivisible integrity of the State with its territory and nation, and to endanger the existence of the democratic and secular order of the Republic based on human rights. In the same article is the stipulation that no provision of the Constitution shall be interpreted in a manner that enables the State or individuals to destroy the fundamental rights and freedoms recognised by the Constitution or to stage an activity with the aim of restricting them more extensively than stated in the Constitution.

Article 174 of the Constitution states that no provision of the Constitution shall be construed or interpreted as rendering unconstitutional the reform laws, which aim to raise Turkish society above the level of contemporary civilisation and to safeguard the secular character of the Republic, and whose provisions were in force on the date of the adoption of the Constitution by referendum.

Amongst the reform laws that pertain to our subject is Law no. 677 'Closure of Dervish Convents and Tombs, the Abolition of the Office of Keeper of Tombs and the Abolition and Prohibition of Certain Titles'. In the framework of this law, all religious brotherhoods, of whatever faith, and the use of any title to do with religious posts were abolished. Any services connected to these institutions and the wearing of garments pertaining to these posts was also prohibited.[60] This law also shut down Alevi places of worship and prevented their leaders from using their religious titles. Both Alevi and other Sunni Islamic groups were banned from having legal personality. This Law has Constitutional protection and cannot be interpreted as unconstitutional in Turkish domestic law. Although it is exceptionally rare for this law to be used in courts to prosecute anyone who uses these titles, the authorities and religious communities consider this to be the reason why the Alevi faith and their places of worship and religious leaders are not legally recognised.[61]

At this point, it will be useful to once again briefly mention the *Diyanet*, which was founded in 1924, as at this moment in Turkey all religious functions are dealt with by the *Diyanet*. It is the *Diyanet* that appoints the clergy and other religious officials that serve all Muslim communities—and there are no exceptions to this rule.[62] According to article 136 of the Constitution of 1982,

> The Presidency of Religious Affairs, which is within the general administration, shall exercise its duties prescribed in its particular law, in accordance with the principles of secularism, removed from all political views and ideas, and aiming at national solidarity and integrity.

As for the Establishment Law of the Presidency of Religious Affairs, it is called the Special Law.[63] Article 7 of this law details its duties. These duties include such tasks as taking decisions on religious matters, issuing opinions, the opening and management of mosques and prayer rooms, the opening of Quranic courses, opening of student hostels and enlightening the public on religious matters through the media and other channels. As is evident from this list, the *Diyanet* has been granted broad powers. Moreover, the *Diyanet* is funded by the State. In the present day, as a result of the Government policy, the authority of the *Diyanet* has increased in all areas of life.[64]

In brief, the *Diyanet* administers Islamic practices in Turkey, while other religions are the responsibility of the General Directorate of Foundations (*Vakıflar Genel Müdürlüğü*).[65] Muslim associations are managed by the *Diyanet*, while Alevis, whose faith is very different to Sunni Islam, claim the *Diyanet* discriminates against them.[66] Hence, as noted by the Venice Commission, in practice there is clear discrimination between Muslims and non-Muslims.[67] In present circumstances, the problems encountered by religious and faith groups with minority status will be examined next under four headings:

5.3.1.1 Planning Regulations
A place of worship does not automatically gain the official status of place of worship when it is established. The necessary permission must be obtained from the relevant authorities. Otherwise, premises that do not have the status of place of worship are unable to benefit from the privileges that premises with this status possess. For instance, bills such as electricity, water and gas may be paid for by the *Diyanet*'s budget. However,

applications for place of worship status by Alevi cemevi, Protestant churches and Jehovah's Witnesses prayer (Kingdom) halls encounter systematic obstacles.

The greatest legal obstacle stems from the Building Law. This law has undergone some reform during the EU membership process. The term 'mosque' in articles 18 and 44 has been replaced by the term 'place of worship', and inserted in the text, in article 9 of Law no. 4928 enacted on 15 July 2003. This was a positive change as places of worship are no longer solely mosques. Also, in supplementary article 2 is the following: "In the drawing up of urban plans sufficient space for necessary places of worship shall be allocated, taking into consideration the circumstances of the district and its future needs." In the same article, it is stated that places of worship may be established on the condition that they have permission from the local authorities and comply with planning regulations.[68]

Despite this significant progress, when the situation in practice is examined, it is evident that the actual utilisation of existing rights has been made almost impossible. It is apparent that the regulations in question are being used to hinder the applications made by non-Muslims for place of worship status. As for Alevis, they are unable to obtain permission from the local authorities.[69] Currently in Turkey there are 948 Alevi cemevi, 52 Jehovah's Witnesses' prayer (Kingdom) halls, 398 churches, 38 synagogues and 3 havra (small synagogue); however, almost all of them do not have legal permission as a place of worship.[70] Instead, they function as associations and foundations.

However, in this regard, the ECtHR handed down a judgment in the case of *Cumhuriyetçi Eğitim ve Kültür Merkezi Vakfi v. Turkey* in 2014, finding a violation of article 9 in conjunction with article 14.[71] In this judgment, the Court found the attitude of the Turkish State to cemevi to be neither objective nor acceptable. In spite of this judgment, the applications of religious minorities to open places of worship continue to be rejected for a variety of reasons.

The refusal of permission for planning is harming social ties between these communities and the State. Furthermore, unfortunately, it is leading to attacks on these groups. As an example of such attacks, in January 2019, there was an explosion at a Protestant church in Mardin in southeast Turkey during a service, causing panic amongst the congregation. Such incidents, particularly the attack referred to in Mardin, do not just affect the targeted congregation, but make Christians elsewhere worry about safety at their places of worship.[72] On 3 May 2018, offensive slogans were daubed on the walls of the Kestel Hacı Bektaş-ı Veli Culture Centre and Cemevi by an unidentified masked person.[73] There has been a significant increase in such hate crimes in recent years.

When you wish to open a mosque in Turkey, you will be obliged to comply with the *Diyanet*'s standards as regards construction. These standards do not in any way take into consideration the needs or material circumstances of religious or faith groups.[74] For instance, İzmir Metropolitan Municipality does not permit places of worship in premises smaller than 2500 square metres in zoning parcels,[75] although, as some faith groups in Turkey have small congregations, they do not need such large premises. Additionally, they do not have the funds to cover construction and maintenance costs. Hence, most of these groups endeavour to provide services by relying on donations from their congregations, without receiving any State assistance.

For instance, Protestants in Turkey explain the process of obtaining permission for places of worship as follows:

> Local government, particularly council authorities who are worried about being seen to be opening churches or allowing churches to open, as it may lose them votes, adopt a negative attitude to requests to establish places of worship. This shows the extent of the problem and the need for a multi-faceted solution.[76]

A report published by the Association of Protestant Churches noted that when applications for places of worship were made, local authorities applied to the *Diyanet* for an opinion. However, the *Diyanet* has no legal right to deliver an opinion on this subject, nor is there a legal obligation for local authorities to apply for such an opinion. In this context, it should be noted that such decisions are under the influence of the *Diyanet*, which conflicts with neutrality principles.[77]

At this juncture, it will be useful to look at Court judgments. For instance, the case opened by the Yenice branch of the *Cem Vakfı* and Sıtkı Baba Cemevi in Tarsus, closely observed by other Alevi associations, on the issue of 'cemevi electricity bills being paid by the State' concluded at the Tarsus no. 1 Court of First Instance. The Court found cemevi should be considered as places of worship and that their electricity bills should be met from the *Diyanet* budget.[78] In particular, this judgment is significant as the effect of the ECtHR judgment in 2014 regarding *CEM Vakfı* can be seen. Following this judgment of the ECtHR, the Court of Cassation in Turkey returned the file to a lower court that had handed down a verdict finding that cemevi were not places of worship. The Court in question reviewed the file and decided the Alevi cemevi electricity bills should be met by the State, rejecting a claim by BEDAŞ (Electricity provider). BEDAŞ appealed the verdict, but the Court of Cassation ratified the judgments, against BEDAŞ.[79]

In brief, the effects of ECtHR judgments on national jurisdiction are important. However, prior to these two judgments, such cases had concluded to the detriment of religious groups on two grounds. Firstly, the opinion of the *Diyanet* was very effective. For instance, in a communication sent by the *Diyanet* to the Ministry of the Interior on 17 December 2004 was the following:

> It is not possible to consider cemevi (cem house) and other places as places of worship because Alevisim, which is a sub-group within Islam, cannot have a place of worship other than mosques and masjid that are common places of worship within Islam.[80]

This opinion of the *Diyanet* has naturally been criticised by Alevis, who see themselves as a separate faith group.[81] The second reason is the law mentioned above (the Law on the Closure of Dervish Lodges and Shrines and the Abolition of the Position of Caretakers of Shrines and Certain Titles).

Hence, prior to 2014 courts were not handing down judgments that recognised places of worship parallel to ECtHR judgments. For instance, in 2012 the Court of Cassation quashed a judgment of a local court that had rejected a case filed to close the Çankaya Cemevi Yaptırma Derneği (Association). The Court found that it was not possible in law for a premise to be accepted as a place of worship unless it was a mosque or Muslim prayer room.[82] In this judgment, the Court did not make any reference to the freedom of religion and belief or consider the proportionality of the effect the refusal to recognise cemevi as a place of worship would have on Alevis.[83]

It will be appropriate to mention another important development in this issue. Following the judgment in the case of the *Cem Vakfi* case, the Turkish Government submitted an action plan to the Committee of Ministers on 23 October 2019. This plan envisaged introducing a planning amnesty for buildings constructed without permission existing in May 2018, including cemevi, requiring applications to be made until June 2019. However, it is not clear whether this amnesty will lead to a change in urban planning or in the title deed of the building. Furthermore, there is an application fee to be paid in order to benefit from the amnesty, and it is stated that this fee will not be met from the *Diyanet* budget. This is something that is not feasible for communities in financial difficulties. Moreover, this amnesty is a temporary solution and does not mean that these premises will be legally registered as places of worship.[84]

To summarise, the ECtHR judgment in the *Cem Vakfi* case has had positive repercussions in Turkish law. A tentative transitional step has even been taken with the zoning amnesty. However, in practice, it is still necessary to obtain permission from the local authority to open a place of worship, and unfortunately, local authorities continue to make the application process difficult. The existing zoning amnesty does not offer a permanent solution in compliance with ECtHR judgments. In the recent period, the People's Republican Party's (*Cumhuriyet Halk Partisi—CHP*) Ekrem İmamoğlu, who was elected mayor of İstanbul after 25 years of rule by the Justice and Development Party (*Adalet ve Kalkınma Partisi—AKP*), proposed that the cleaning and other services to cemevi would be provided by the İstanbul Metropolitan Municipality (*İstanbul Büyükşehir Belediyesi—İBB*) and that they would be granted legal status. His proposal was rejected by a majority of city councillors from the AKP and MHP (*Milliyetçi Hareket Partisi—Nationalist Action Party*) on 16 January 2020.[85] However, on 14 January 2020, the İzmir Metropolitan Municipality, which has a majority of CHP councillors, voted to permit cemevi to be recognised as places of worship in urban planning. This decision was welcomed by representatives of the Alevi-Bektaşi community.[86] However, there are concerns that the decision may be rejected by the city governor. Peoples' Democracy Party (*Halkların Demokratik Partisi—HDP*) MP Ali Kenanoğlu has stated that it is highly likely that the governor's office will annul this decision.[87]

5.3.1.2 *Legal Personality*

Another problem faced by religious minority groups in Turkey is the fact they are unable to gain legal personality. This is naturally a significant obstacle in their establishing places of worship and providing services. At the present time, religious minorities carry out activities by means of associations and foundations, but this does not grant them sufficient legal status. As they do not have legal status, they cannot own their property. Additionally, they cannot benefit from the *Diyanet* budget or the services of local authorities. For instance, legally, bills such as those for electricity may be met by the *Diyanet* budget, but in practice does not take place. Furthermore, while technically the salaries of religious or faith groups should be paid by the *Diyanet*, as these groups do not have legal status, they are unable to benefit from these privileges.[88]

For instance, as all cemevi and most churches are not recognised as places of worship, occasionally the police or local authority do not recognise their right of tenancy. For instance, the Latin Catholic Community in Turkey cannot own property in their name, nor can they go to court as they have no legal personality. Consequently, the Latin Catholic Community endeavours to overcome problems through the political negotiations of the Holy See and the Turkish authorities.[89]

The Government, in line with the Treaty of Lausanne, has only given permission for the Greek, Armenian and Jewish minorities to open places of worship. For instance, it has given permission for the Ahtamar church in Van to be restored to allow its use by the Armenian Apostolic community. Permission has also been given for a Greek Orthodox Church in the Sümela Monastery in Trabzon.[90]

It is also necessary to say that according to article 101(4) of the Turkish Civil Code, no foundation may establish a trust for the purpose of supporting a community. However, in the case of *Altınkaynak and others v. Turkey*, the ECtHR announced its judgment on 15 January 2019, finding that article 11 of the ECHR, dealing with the freedom of association, had been violated by the failure to permit the establishing of a foundation by applicants belonging to the Seventh Day Adventists faith. This judgment is significant since it is the first to address this rule directly.[91]

Despite this judgment of the ECtHR in 2019, at the time this article was penned, no changes had been made to the Turkish Civil Code. Apart from this, in 2013, the General Directorate of Foundations revoked the articles in its regulations governing the election of management boards by community trusts themselves, indicating that new provisions would be introduced. However, since no new provisions have been made, these foundations are unable to carry out any elections, which restricts their freedom of association. Hence, due to death, resignation or for other reasons, these foundations are experiencing a reduction in management board member numbers, causing serious problems in foundation activities. The General Directorate of Foundations sent a notification to regional directorates on 11 March 2019, instructing them to allow foundations with management boards with diminishing numbers of members to appoint members to boards, which is not a democratic manner of management. The current situation is one where members or supporters of these foundations have had their democratic right to hold an election taken away from them. This constitutes a serious interference in the right of these communities to associate and organise freely.[92]

5.3.1.3 The Appointment of Religious Leaders

The autonomy or freedom in internal affairs of religious or faith communities includes the right to appoint their own religious leaders.[93]

The law that came into force in 1925, 'Closure of Dervish Convents and Tombs, the Abolition of the Office of Keeper of Tombs and the Abolition and Prohibition of Certain Titles', banned titles and services such as dervish, novicehood, sorcerer, fortune teller and exorcist.[94] In this context, it is important to examine the ECtHR Grand Chamber judgment in the case of *İzzettin Doğan and others v. Turkey*.[95] As mentioned above, this case concerns the failure of the authorities to provide the religious services requested by the Alevi applicants as public services. In other words, the non-recognition of the Alevi community leads to Alevis being unable to effectively exercise their rights to freely manifest their religion or faith.[96] On account of this denial of rights, the Alevi community is unable to gain acceptance of their places of worship, the cemevi, as legally recognised places of worship. This renders it impossible for their religious leaders, called '*dede*', to use their titles. In this case, the Grand Chamber concluded that there had been a violation of article 9, finding that the State had exceeded the margin of appreciation in not submitting valid and sufficient grounds for its actions. Consequently, the intervention that was the subject of the complaint was not considered necessary in a democratic society. Additionally, a violation was also found of article 14 taken in conjunction with article 9 on account of there being no objective and reasonable grounds for the treatment to which Alevis had been subjected.

In the action plan that Turkey submitted to the Council of Ministers on 8 February 2017, it was stated that work was ongoing in order to take the necessary measures by considering the demands of applicants so that no such violations would occur.[97] However, it is not clear with which sections of society information was shared during the evaluation process. Whereas, the *İzzettin Doğan and others* judgment presented a significant opportunity to engage in a process of consultation with all sections of society, not just the Alevis, to implement reform of legislation dealing with religious services provided as public services by observing obligations concerning human rights law and the principle of impartiality and equality. In this context, it should be noted that although a significant proportion of society benefits from the religious services provided by the *Diyanet*, some segments of society do not and some complain, and these services are paid for by the taxes of all citizens.[98]

Hence, apart from Alevis, Sunni Muslim communities also do not have a say in the appointment of their religious leaders. Sometimes, a religious official the congregation of a mosque do not want may be appointed as imam by the *Diyanet*. It is not possible for any community to participate in the appointment process. The Armenian Apostolic, Jewish and Greek Orthodox communities experience the same problems. For instance, the Armenian Apostolic community wished to replace the 84th Patriarch, Mesrob Mutafyan, in 2008, when he fell ill, with an assistant. Subsequently, they were unable to freely carry out an election for a successor, in spite of applying to the Interior Ministry via the İstanbul Governor's office. As a result of State intervention, in 2010 an Acting Patriarch was appointed. In February 2018, the İstanbul Governor's office intervened in the election process by sending a notification to the effect that Patriarch Mutafyan was still alive, that the Acting Patriarch Aram Ateşyan was still in his post and that conditions for an election did not exist, thus preventing an election taking place.[99] The Protestant Churches Association has stated that in the last two years around 100 members of the clergy who are foreign citizens have had to leave Turkey on account of visas or residence permits not being renewed.[100] Since it is also not possible for educational institutions for religious officials to be established, naturally they are brought in from abroad. In this context, it is of the utmost importance that these religious officials are granted visas or residence permits. The case of Pastor Andrew Brunson, which led to a serious crisis between the United States of America (USA) and Turkey, is a good recent example. Pastor Brunson was remanded in prison for two years and, after being released, was sent back to the USA.[101,102]

In conclusion, religious and faith communities face restrictions regarding electing and appointing their leaders. There is therefore a need for a participatory process within the structure of the *Diyanet* for the appointment of religious leaders.[103]

5.3.1.4 Teaching
International law safeguards the right to teach the freedom of religion and belief. This may take place in religious schools and seminaries. However, in Turkey, the dissemination of a religion or belief different to that of the majority is looked on with suspicion. For example, since 2016, the

Diyarbakır Metropolitan Municipality has not permitted the Diyarbakır Protestant Church to participate in festivals with Christian materials. In 2018, the Üsküdar Church in İstanbul was unable to obtain permission from the Üsküdar Municipality for a stall dispensing public information.[104]

The State has a monopoly on the founding of institutions that provide religious instruction. Article 24 of the Turkish Constitution states:

> Education and instruction in religion and ethics shall be conducted under State supervision and control. Instruction in religious culture and moral education shall be compulsory in the curricula of primary and secondary schools. Other religious education and instruction shall be subject to the individual's own desire, and in the case of minors, to the request of their legal representatives.

According to the Law on Private Schools, the opening of religious schools is not permitted and public schools that offer religious education in Islam must follow Ministry of National Education curricula. The Halki Theological Seminary, belonging to the Ecumenical Patriarchate, has not been open since 1971, which demonstrates the State's blanket prohibition of the opening of institutions for the training of clergy and other religious officials by any group. Another example of this ban is the Turkish authorities ignoring a 2002 request by the Armenian Apostolic Church to open a training institute for clergy and other religious officials under the auspices of the General Directorate of Higher Education. The State's failure to reply to the request effectively blocked it. The Apostolic Church's Holy Cross Seminary had been closed down by the State in 1971.[105]

5.4 Conclusion

While the origins of problems relating to minority religions and faith groups in Turkey can be traced back to the Ottoman era, the founding of the Republic unfortunately did not result in these problems being seriously resolved. Hate crimes directed towards these minorities in recent times are ominous. As mentioned in other chapters, although in the Constitution the State is said to be secular, in practice, the tie of citizenship has been defined by Turkishness and Islam. In this context, while the *Diyanet* should take a neutral approach to all religions, it has adopted a role that promotes Sunni Islam while constantly marginalising other religious and faith groups. Only the Armenians, Greeks and Jews were granted protection by the Treaty of Lausanne, and in practice, we cannot claim that these groups have been completely safeguarded. However, we may at least say that as regards opening their own places of worship and serving their own communities they have advantages compared to other minority religious and faith groups. For instance, the Alevis face constant exclusion and discrimination. Although they are able to open places of worship (cemevi) through associations or foundations, since these cemevi are not recognised as places of worship, they cannot benefit from state aid. Additionally, as these faith groups do not have legal personality, they cannot freely elect their own representatives. Apart from this, they do not have judicial protection and are even unable to own their properties. There are also restrictions in place regarding their rights to teach their religions by opening schools and seminaries or by other means.

This is the case despite Turkey having been involved in negotiations to join the EU since 2005. As can be seen in reports, the EU calls on Turkey to protect in law and in practice human rights and freedoms for everyone without discrimination. However, despite reforms having been made in both the Constitution and other legislation during the EU process, as can be observed from the examples given above, both the courts and other administrative authorities make decisions that violate rights and freedoms. As stated in article 90(5) of the Constitution, it is necessary for international human rights conventions to be applied in domestic law, as the State has a positive obligation in this regard. States must not restrict these rights and freedoms on the grounds of margin of appreciation. In the EU Progress Report of 2019, it was noted that Turkey had not implemented the plan for cemevi it had submitted to the Committee of Ministers.[106]

The construction of places of worship, their licensing and determining of suitable sites in urban planning, the recognition of place of worship status and freedom of religion and belief should be facilitated in compliance with standards and implemented in a non-discriminatory manner. Furthermore, with regard to place of worship status, the ECtHR judgments should be speedily and effectively implemented. The rights of religious or faith communities to obtain legal personality should be protected in line with international human rights norms. In particular, the sentence in article 101 of the Turkish Civil Code, "A foundation cannot be established for the purpose of supporting members of certain…communities" should be removed. The regulations for associations and foundations should be reviewed and improved to comply with standards governing the freedom of association and the freedom of belief and religion. Furthermore, the election and appointment of religious officials is an internal matter for religious or faith communities, and there should be no question of interference in internal affairs. The necessary, accessible and non-discriminatory provisions should be introduced to ensure it is possible for these communities in Turkey to invite and employ foreign religious officials. The regulations on elections for community foundations should be drawn up with urgency following a participatory process.[107] Finally, the relevant provisions should be introduced so that the teaching of religion and belief is safeguarded in compliance with article 9 of the ECHR. This right should include being able to open institutions where communities can train their own clergy.[108]

Notes

1. The CIA World Factbook states that the population of Turkey is around 82 million, 99.8% of whom identify as Muslim. And 77.5% of them see themselves as Sunni. The number of people who identify as Alevi varies between 10 and 25 million, but the Turkish Government does not recognise them as a minority different from the majority Sunni Muslims. The other 0.2% of the population is made up of atheists, Armenian Apostolics, Bahá'ís, Bulgarian Orthodox, Chaldean Catholics, Greek Orthodox, Jehovah's Witnesses, Jews, Protestants, Roman Catholics, Syriac Catholics, Syriac Orthodox and other religious groups (see International Religious Freedom Reports, (2019), 'Turkey: USCIRF–Recommended for Special Watch List', p. 83, https://www.uscirf.gov/sites/default/files/Turkey.pdf, accessed 21 September 2020).
2. European Commission, (2019), 'Turkey 2019 Report', p. 39, https://ec.europa.eu/neighbourhood-enlargement/sites/near/files/20190529-turkey-report.pdf, accessed 21 September 2020.
3. M. Yıldırım, 'A Trapped Right: The Right to Have Places of Worship in Turkey', in Ö. H. Çınar and M. Yıldırım, *Freedom of Religion and Belief in Turkey* (Newcastle upon Tyne: Cambridge Scholars Publishing, 2014), p. 165, footnote 11.
4. HRC, General Comment no. 22, 'The Right to Freedom of Thought, Conscience and Religion', UN Doc. CCPR/C/21/Rev.1/Add.4, 30 July 1993, para. 4.
5. G. A. Öncü, *Özel Yaşama ve Aile Yaşamına Saygı Hakkı* (Ankara: Anayasa Mahkemesi Yayınları, 2019), p. 154.

6. U. Kilkelly, *The right to respect for private and family life: A guide to the implementation of Article 8 of the European Convention on Human Rights* (Strasbourg: Council of Europe, 2003), p. 25.
7. *Silver and Others v. United Kingdom*, 25 March 1983, Nos. 5947/72; 6205/73; 7052/75; 7061/75; 7107/75; 7113/75; 7136/75, para. 90.
8. *Open Door Counsel – ling v. Ireland*, 29 October 1992, No. 14234/88.
9. Kilkelly, *supra note* 6, p. 30.
10. *Olsson v. Sweden*, 24 March 1988, No. 10465/83, para. 67.
11. *Coster v. United Kingdom*, 18 January 2001, No. 24876/94, para. 104; *Jane Smith v. United Kingdom (GC)*, 18 January 2001, No. 25154/94, para. 54.
12. *Handyside v. United Kingdom*, 7 December 1976, No. 5493/72, para. 49.
13. Ibid., para. 48.
14. Ibid., para. 11.
15. *Olsson v. Sweden (No. 2)*, 30 October 1992, No. 13441/87, para. 91.
16. Kilkelly, *supra note* 6, p. 32.
17. Council of Europe, *Guide on Article 9 of the European Convention on Human Rights* (Strasbourg: Council of Europe, 2020), pp. 16–20.
18. Kilkelly, *supra note* 6, p. 21.
19. *Beganovic v. Croatia*, 25 June 2009, No. 46423/96; *Storck v. Germany*, 16 June 2005, No. 61603/00.
20. O. Doğru and A. Nalbant, *İnsan Hakları Avrupa Sözleşmesi Açıklama ve Önemli Kararlar* (Strasbourg: Council of Europe, 2. Volume, 2013), pp. 128–131.
21. *The Church of Jesus Christ of Latter-Day Saints v. United Kingdom*, 4 March 2014, No. 7552/09, para. 30; *Cumhuriyetçi Eğitim ve Kültür Merkezi Vakfı v. Turkey*, 2 December 2014, No. 32093/10, para. 41.
22. *Association de solidarité avec les témoins de Jéhovah and Others v. Turkey*, 17 July 2016, Nos. 36915/10 and 8606/13, para. 90.
23. Council of Europe, *supra note* 17, p. 44.
24. *Association de solidarité avec les témoins de Jéhovah and Others v. Turkey*, *supra note* 22, para. 97.
25. *Juma Mosque Congregation and Others v. Azerbaijan*, 8 January 2013, No. 15405/04, para. 60.
26. *Religious Community of Jehovah's Witnesses of Kryvyi Rih's Ternivsky District v. Ukraine*, 3 September 2019, No. 21477/10, para. 53.
27. *Rymsko-Katolytska Gromada Svyatogo Klimentiya v. Misti Sevastopoli v. Ukraine*, 3 May 2016, No. 22607/02, paras. 59–63.
28. *Gromada Ukrayinskoyi Greko-Katolitskoyi Tserkvy Sela Korshiv v. Ukraine*, 3 May 2016, No.9557/04, paras. 33–38.

29. *Cumhuriyetçi Eğitim ve Kültür Merkezi Vakfı v. Turkey, supra note* 21, paras. 48–49.
30. *Association de solidarité avec les témoins de Jéhovah and Others v. Turkey, supra note* 22, para. 103; *Religious Community of Jehovah's Witnesses of Kryvyi Rih's Ternivsky District v. Ukraine, supra note* 26, para. 51.
31. *Association de solidarité avec les témoins de Jéhovah and Others v. Turkey, supra note* 22, para. 95.
32. Ibid., para. 103.
33. Ibid., para. 105.
34. *Manoussakis and Others v. Greece*, 26 September 1996, No. 18748/91.
35. *Tanyar and Küçükergin v. Turkey*, 5 December 2006, No. 74242/01. Also see Doğru and Nalbant, *supra note* 20, p. 128.
36. *Cumhuriyetçi Eğitim ve Kültür Merkezi Vakfı v. Turkey, supra note* 21, paras. 53–54.
37. Norwegian Helsinki Committee, the Freedom of Belief Initiative, and Forum 18, (2019), 'Turkey UPR submission, July 2019', para. 24, https://inancozgurlugugirisimi.org/wp-content/uploads/2020/01/NHC-IOG-F18-UPR-Turkey-submission-2019-2.pdf, accessed 21 September 2020.
38. *Masaev v. Moldova*, 12 May 2009, No. 6303/05, para. 26.
39. *Dimitrova v. Bulgaria*, 27 January 2011, No. 44862/04. Also see Council of Europe, *supra note* 17, p. 42.
40. *Serif v. Greece*, 14 March 2000, No. 38178/97.
41. Ibid., para. 13.
42. Ibid., para. 53.
43. *Hasan and Chaush v. Bulgaria*, 26 October 2000, No. 30985/96.
44. Ibid., para. 62.
45. *Metropolitan Church of Bessarabia and Others v. Moldova*, 13 December 2001, No. 45701/99, para. 118.
46. For instance, *Fener Rum Erkek Lisesi Vafkı v. Türkiye*, 9 January 2007, No. 34478/97; *Apostolidi vd. v. Turkey*, 27 March 2007, No. 45628/99; *Fener Rum Patriarchate v. Turkey*, 8 July 2008, No. 14340/05; *Yedikule Surp Pirgiç Ermeni Hastanesi Vakfı v. Turkey*, 16 December 2008, No. 36165/02; *Samatya Surp Kervok Ermeni Kilisesi, Mektebi ve Mezarlığı Vakfı Yötenim Kurulu v. Turkey*, 16 December 2008, No. 1480/03; *Bozcaada Kimisis Teodoku Rum Ortodoks Kilisesi Vakfı v. Turkey no. 2*, 3 March 2009, Nos. 37639/03, 37655/03, 26736/04 and 42670/04.
47. TBMM Araştırma Merkezi, (2006), *Venedik Komisyonu: Türkiye'ye İlişkin Görüşleri Seçimler Yargı ve Referanduma İlişkin Karar ve Uygulama Kodları*, pp. 49–50, https://www.tbmm.gov.tr/yayinlar/venedik_komisyonu.pdf, accessed on 21 September 2020.
48. European Commission, *supra note* 2, p. 39.

49. *Liga van Moskeeën en Islamitische Organisaties Provincie Antwerpen and Others*, 29 May 2018, C-426/16, EU:C:2018:335, para. 44; *Jehovan todistajat*, 10 July 2018, C-25/17, EU:C:2018:551, para. 47.
50. *Secure Solutions*, 14 March 2017, G4S C-157/15, EU:C:2017:203, para. 28; *Bougnauoi and ADDH*, 14 March 2017, C-188/15, EU:C:2017:204, para. 30.
51. European Commission, *supra note* 2, pp. 44–45.
52. Council of Europe, 'Opinion on the Legal Status of Religious Communities in Turkey and the Right of the Orthodox Patriarchate of İstanbul to use the adjective "Ecumenical" adopted by the Venice Commission at its 82nd Plenary Session' (Venice, 12–13 March 2010), pp. 19–20, https://www.venice.coe.int/webforms/documents/?pdf=CDL-AD(2010)005-e, accessed 21 September 2020.
53. H. Karababa, *Sivas Davası* (İstanbul: Ilkim, 2008), p. 12.
54. Yıldırım, *supra note* 3, p. 179, footnotes 23 and 24.
55. International Religious Freedom Reports, *supra note* 1, p. 83.
56. Ibid.
57. Presidency of the Republic of Turkey (2019), 'Presidential Spokesperson İbrahim Kalın's Statement on the Turkey Chapter of the 2019 Annual Report of the U.S. Commission on International Religious Freedom', https://www.tccb.gov.tr/en/spokesperson/1696/105205/presidential-spokesperson-ibrahim-kalin-s-statement-on-the-turkey-chapter-of-the-2019-annual-report-of-the-u-s-commission-on-international-religious-freedom, accessed 21 September 2020.
58. H. S. Demir, *Türkiye'de Din ve Vicdan Özgürlüğü* (Ankara: Adalet Yayınevi, 2011), pp. 106–108.
59. Turkish Constitutional Court, 4 November 1986, E. 1986/11, K. 1986/26.
60. Closure of Dervish Convents and Tombs, the Abolition of the Office of Keeper of Tombs and the Abolition and Prohibition of Certain Titles, Law no. 677, adopted 30 November 1925, Official gazette dated 13 December 1925 (No. 243).
61. Norwegian Helsinki Committee and Forum 18, *supra note* 37, para. 36.
62. Ibid., para. 37.
63. The Establishment Law of the Presidency of Religious Affairs, Law no. 633, adopted 22 June 1965, Official gazette dated 2 July 1965 (No. 12038).
64. European Commission, *supra note* 2, p. 36. Also see B. Özenç, 'The Religion Box on Identity Cards as a Means to Understand the Turkish Type of Secularism', in Çınar and Yıldırım, *supra note* 3, pp. 105–107; İ. Gözaydın, 'Management of Religion in Turkey: They Diyanet and Beyond', in Çınar and Yıldırım, *supra note* 3, pp. 10–26.

65. International Religious Freedom Reports, *supra note* 1, p. 2.
66. Tunca Öğreten, 'The Alevis' fight for recognition in Turkey', *DW*, 26 January 2020, https://www.dw.com/en/the-alevis-fight-for-recognition-in-turkey/a-52154523, accessed 21 September 2020.
67. TBMM Araştırma Merkezi, *supra note* 47, p. 57.
68. The Building Law, Law no. 3194, adopted 3 May 1985, Official gazette dated 9 May 1985 (No. 18749), supplementary article 2.
69. Norwegian Helsinki Committee İnanç Özgürlüğü Girişimi, (2014), 'Alevi cem evleri: Türkiye ve Din veya İnanç Özgürlüğü Toplumsal tartışmaya katkı', p. 4, https://inancozgurlugugirisimi.org/wp-content/uploads/2014/04/NHCIOG_PolicyPaper_Alevi-tr-final.pdf, accessed 21 September 2020.
70. 'Hangi ilde kaç cemevi var?', *Haber7com*, 16 March 2013, http://www.haber7.com/guncel/haber/1002426-hangi-ilde-kac-cemevi-var-liste, accessed 21 September 2020; Yıldırım, *supra note* 3, p. 169; 'Dünya Çapındaki Yehova'nın Şahitleri: Türkiye', https://www.jw.org/tr/yehovanin-sahitleri/dunya-capinda/TR/, accessed 21 September 2020; 'Türkiye'de Hristiyan ve Yahudilere ait 439 ibadethane ve 24 dernek var', *Independent Türkçe*, 5 November 2019, https://www.indyturk.com/node/88486/haber/t%C3%BCrkiye%E2%80%99de-hristiyan-ve-yahudilere-ait-439-ibadethane-ve-24-dernek-var, accessed 21 September 2020.
71. *Cumhuriyetçi Eğitim ve Kültür Merkezi Vakfı v. Turkey*, *supra note* 21.
72. Norwegian Helsinki Committee and Forum 18, *supra note* 37, para. 23.
73. Norwegian Helsinki Committee İnanç Özgürlüğü Girişimi, (2019), 'Hak ve Eşitliğin Peşinde Türkiye'de İnanç Özgürlüğü Hakkını İzleme Raporu Ocak 2016 – Mart 2019', p. 17, https://inancozgurlugugirisimi.org/wp-content/uploads/2019/07/Report_Turkey_web.pdf, accessed 21 September 2020.
74. Yıldırım, *supra note* 3, p. 170.
75. İzmir Greater City Municipality Public Works Regulation, Article 84, revised on 12 April 2013.
76. Yıldırım, *supra note* 3, p. 170, footnote 41.
77. Ibid., p. 170, footnotes 42 and 43.
78. 'Mahkeme kararı: "Cemevleri ibadethanedir, elektrik faturası Diyanet tarafından ödenecek"', *Haber Türk*, 12 December 2018, https://www.haberturk.com/mahkeme-karari-cemevleri-ibadethanedir-elektrik-faturasi-diyanet-tarafindan-odenecek-2257690, accessed 21 September 2020.
79. 'Yargıtay: Cemevleri ibadethanedir, faturalarını devlet karşılamalı', *Gazete Duvar*, 27 November 2018, https://www.gazeteduvar.com.tr/gun-

dem/2018/11/27/yargitay-cemevleri-ibadethanedir-faturalarini-devlet-karsilamali/, accessed 21 September 2020.
80. Yıldırım, *supra note* 3, p. 172, footnote 49.
81. Ibid., footnote 50.
82. 'Yargıtay cemevine kapıyı kapattı: İbadethane değil', *Radikal*, 25 Temmuz 2012, http://www.radikal.com.tr/turkiye/yargitay-cemevine-kapiyi-kapatti-ibadethane-degil-1095215/.
83. Yıldırım, *supra note* 3, pp. 173–174.
84. Council of Europe, Committee of Ministers, 7 November 2019, DH-DD(2019)1294, pp. 7–8, https://rm.coe.int/090000168098b4a8, accessed 21 September 2020.
85. 'İBB Meclis Çoğunluğu Cemevine İbadethane Statüsü Vermedi', *İstanbul Büyükşehir Belediyesi*, 16 January 2020, https://www.ibb.istanbul/News/Detail/36340, accessed 21 September 2020.
86. 'İzmir'de cemevleri imar planlarına ibadethane olarak yazılacak', *İzmir Büyükşehir Belediyesi*, 14 January 2020, https://www.izmir.bel.tr/tr/Haberler/izmirde-cemevleri-imar-planlarina-ibadethane-olarak-yazilacak/41213/156, accessed 21 September 2020.
87. Menekse Tokyay, 'Cemevlerine İbadethane Statüsü: 'Sihirli Formül' nedir?', *Euronews*, 18 January 2020, https://tr.euronews.com/2020/01/18/cemevlerine-ibadethane-statusu-sihirli-formul-nedir, accessed 21 September 2020.
88. Yıldırım, *supra note* 3, pp. 174–175, footnotes 78–82.
89. Ibid., footnotes 81–82.
90. Ibid., footnotes 83–85.
91. *Altınkaynak and others v. Turkey*, 15 January 2019, No. 12541/06. Also see Norwegian Helsinki Committee İnanç Özgürlüğü Girişimi, *supra note* 73, p. 33.
92. Ibid., p. 34.
93. HRC General Comment no. 22, *supra note* 4, para. 4.
94. Norwegian Helsinki Committee İnanç Özgürlüğü Girişimi, *supra note* 73, p. 89.
95. *İzzettin Doğan and Others v. Turkey (GC)*, 26 April 2016, No. 62649/10.
96. Norwegian Helsinki Committee İnanç Özgürlüğü Girişimi, *supra note* 73, p. 90.
97. Ibid., p. 91.
98. Ibid., pp. 30–32.
99. Ibid., p. 92.
100. Ibid., p. 93.
101. Ibid., p. 94.
102. Ibid., pp. 30–32, footnotes 88–94.
103. Ibid., p. 5.

104. Norwegian Helsinki Committee and Forum 18, *supra note* 37, para. 29.
105. Ibid., para. 32.
106. European Commission, *supra note* 2, p. 32.
107. Norwegian Helsinki Committee İnanç Özgürlüğü Girişimi, *supra note* 73, pp. 42–44.
108. Norwegian Helsinki Committee and Forum 18, *supra note* 37, paras. 33–34.

CHAPTER 6

The Manifestation of Religious Belief in the Public Sphere: Religious Symbols and Dress

Abstract This chapter begins by analysing the current international standards regarding the implementation of freedom of thought, conscience and religion in relation to the manifestation of religion or belief in the public sphere, particularly in relation to the use of religious symbols and dress. This is still a controversial issue in Turkey because the implementation of this freedom has been erratic at best. This chapter will examine the Turkish law and the judgments made by domestic courts. Such a study is also important in order to understand what the international obligations of Turkey are.

Keywords Freedom of religion • Manifestation • Public sphere • Religious symbols and dress • Turkey • International and domestic/national law • *Forum externum*

6.1 Introduction

The freedom of thought, conscience and religion is one of the inalienable freedoms of a democratic society.[1] The manifestation of religion or freedom of belief in the public sphere generally occurs with the use of religious symbols, something which is one of the most controversial topics in Europe.[2] This debate has centred around the issue of the headscarf in particular, on occasions regarding whether a student may go to school wearing a headscarf or whether a public servant may perform her duties in

© The Author(s), under exclusive license to Springer Nature Switzerland AG 2021
Ö. H. Çınar, *Freedom of Religion and Belief in Turkey*,
https://doi.org/10.1007/978-3-030-70077-5_6

115

a headscarf. Of course, this issue cannot be reduced to merely a debate on the headscarf, since there has also been controversy over a Christian wearing a crucifix to work or a Sikh wearing a turban or having long hair and a beard. In particular, the question of whether individuals may worship in working hours has also been a subject of debate amongst academics, politicians and non-governmental organisations as well as in national and international judicial organs.

This issue has been on the agenda in Turkey for years. Turkey acknowledges this freedom in principle through international treaty commitments. However, the implementation of this freedom has been erratic at best. The Justice and Development Party (*Adalet ve Kalkınma Partisi—AKP*) has made some important legal changes in conformity with the political criteria of the European Union (EU), but many restrictions related to the freedom of thought, conscience and religion remain unaddressed. For instance, despite the fact that there is a recent recognition of the headscarf for public servants, there still remain legal, social (e.g. the effects of secularism) and political obstacles for the manifestation of religious belief for public servants at State institutions (e.g. to use religious symbols and to pray during working hours). For instance, a Jewish man cannot wear a kippah (brimless cap).

Hence, the use of symbols or the manifestation of religious belief was for a long time seen as a great threat to secularism and modernism and was not debated within the framework of the freedom of religion and belief. This threat is still raised from time to time. The fact that the headscarf was banned until very recently is the most blatant example of this. The use of religious symbols by public servants while on duty was even banned by legal provisions such as the regulation pertaining to the Dress of Personnel working in Public Sector Institutions. The wearing of headscarves by public servants after work or their participation in religious ceremonies was also seen as contrary to the notion that public servants should set an example to society, and some public servants were prosecuted and convicted.[3] Such measures that began as a violation of the freedom of thought, conscience and religion also led to violations of fundamental rights and freedoms, such as the right to education, the right to work, the right to take part in social life and the right to equality.[4]

In this respect, it is necessary to answer the question as to how the use of religious dress and/or symbols in the public sphere is covered in international law. Therefore, an examination of how the freedom of thought, conscience and religion, which includes the use of religious dress and/or symbols, is safeguarded by international conventions and relevant judgments of the European Court of Human Rights (ECtHR) will be put under the microscope. Such a study is important in order to understand what international obligations Turkey has. In this respect, this chapter will also examine the Turkish Law and the judgments made by domestic courts.

6.2 International Law Standards

The freedom of thought, conscience and religion currently in modern human rights law is recognised in article 18 of the Universal Declaration of Human Rights (UDHR), article 18 of the International Covenant on Civil and Political Rights (ICCPR) and article 9 of the European Convention on Human Rights (ECHR).

These articles consist of two parts. The first part guarantees everyone's right to freedom of thought, conscience and religion. The second part of the article gives a two-pronged definition of the right to freedom of thought, conscience and religion. The first prong makes reference to "freedom to change his religion or belief" and the second mentions "freedom, either alone or in community with others and in public or private, to manifest his religion or belief in teaching, practice, worship and observance". In other words, the first prong of the definition concerns the internal sphere of this right, the *forum internum*. The State has no place in the *forum internum*.[5] The second concerns the external sphere of that right, the *forum externum*, which is subject to some limitations.[6] The manifestation of religion or belief falls within the *forum externum*.

The UDHR has certain general limitation provisions on human rights and freedoms in articles 29 and 30.[7] In the case of article 9 of the ECHR, the *forum externum* (freedom to manifest one's religion or beliefs) may be limited by domestic law in particular circumstances. Therefore, the second paragraph of article 9 sets out some grounds for limiting the right to manifest a religion or belief.[8] The applicant must firstly prove the lack of the first requirement of 'prescribed by law'. The applicant must also prove that no legitimate aims—the interests of 'public safety',[9] 'protection of public order',[10] 'health and morals'[11] or 'the protection of the rights and freedom of others'[12] to interfere with his/her right exist. The applicant must finally prove that the measure was not 'necessary in a democratic society'.[13]

Despite the fact that States enjoy a certain 'margin of appreciation' in terms of interference with the enjoyment of the applicant's right, they do not have 'unlimited power of appreciation'.[14] They are therefore obliged to explain the need for interference in the manifestation of religion or belief in accordance with the article 9(2) limitation clause. Aside from article 9(2), article 15 can also be used to justify the limitation of Convention rights.[15]

In addition to these three main documents, there are also other international conventions that safeguard the freedom of religion and religious belief. Article 7 of the Helsinki Final Act accepted in 1975 states: "Within this framework the participating States will recognize and respect the freedom of the individual to profess and practice, alone or in community with others, religion or belief acting in accordance with the dictates of his own conscience."[16]

In 1981, the Declaration on the Elimination of All Forms of Intolerance and of Discrimination Based on Religion or Belief was accepted by the General Assembly of the United Nations (UN).[17] Article 6 of this Declaration frames the content of the freedom of thought, conscience and religion, thus:

> (a) To worship or assemble in connection with a religion or belief, and to establish and maintain places for these purposes;
>
> (b) To establish and maintain appropriate charitable or humanitarian institutions;
>
> (c) To make, acquire and use to an adequate extent the necessary articles and materials related to the rites or customs of a religion or belief;
>
> (d) To write, issue and disseminate relevant publications in these areas;
>
> (e) To teach a religion or belief in places suitable for these purposes;
>
> (f) To solicit and receive voluntary financial and other contributions from individuals and institutions;
>
> (g) To train, appoint, elect or designate by succession appropriate leaders called for by the requirements and standards of any religion or belief;
>
> (h) To observe days of rest and to celebrate holidays and ceremonies in accordance with the precepts of one's religion or belief;
>
> (i) To establish and maintain communications with individuals and communities in matters of religion and belief at the national and international levels.

The Human Rights Committee (HRC) has with its observations endeavoured to broaden the scope of safeguarded freedoms. In its 22nd General Comment in 1993, the HRC gave the broadest possible meaning to the terms 'religion' and 'belief'. In paragraph 4 of the same comment, it was stated that the use of symbols should be included within the scope of worship, as should the wearing of faith-related clothing while not performing religious rites and the covering of the head.

In 2005, the UN Commission on Human Rights, in its decision no. 2005/40, made the following recommendation to States:

> To exert the utmost efforts, in accordance with their national legislation and in conformity with international human rights law, to ensure that religious places, sites, shrines and religious expressions are fully respected and protected and to take additional measures in cases where they are vulnerable to desecration or destruction.[18]

In short, the freedom of thought, conscience and religion—in which freedom of belief must be included—is one of the fundamental freedoms in international human rights law defined as non-derogable. Not only religious beliefs but also non-religious beliefs such as atheism, for instance, are also safeguarded. People may exercise these freedoms alone or in groups. In the event of groups exercising this freedom, States have to respect the autonomy of these groups and respect their right to elect their own leaders and teachers and to set up their own schools. People may also use various symbols in their worship, and it is necessary for the scope of these symbols to be broad.[19] Hence, a person's use of dress in accordance with their religion or belief in the public sphere is safeguarded by international law and a person's right to a religion or belief and to change is accepted as *forum internum*. Therefore, States cannot intervene in this sphere. However, the manifestation of religion or belief is accepted as *forum externum*, which is subject to restrictions. While such restrictions are necessary in a democratic society, they must conform to the principle of proportionality. International human rights law also stipulates that discrimination based on religion or belief is unacceptable.

6.2.1   The European Court of Human Rights' Case Law

The obligations of Turkey regarding the freedom of thought, conscience and religion in international documents are clear. How the ECtHR interprets this freedom, in particular the use of religious symbols in the public sphere, will offer significant insight as regards the domestic judicial systems in Turkey. Hence, since Turkey is a member of the Council of Europe, how the ECtHR interprets this freedom will be examined in this chapter.

The ECtHR has addressed the question of bans on the use of religious dress and/or symbols in the public sphere.[20] Until its abolition in 1998, the European Commission of Human Rights made judgments on these issues.[21] For instance, in a judgment in 1981, *Ahmad v. United Kingdom*, the Commission examined the case of a teacher who had resigned after the school administration had not approved his request to leave his post 45 minutes early in order to go to the mosque on Fridays.[22] The Commission noted that the applicant had made no such request when taking up his post or during the first six years, when he had knowingly accepted these conditions without coercion and that by resigning would be able to find a job appropriate to his beliefs. The Commission, therefore, found that there had been no violation of article 9 of the Convention. The Commission maintained the same stance in the case of *Stedman v. United Kingdom*.[23] In this case, the applicant, a Christian, was sometimes obliged to work on a Sunday. The Commission found this application inadmissible, basing its decision on similar grounds as in the *Ahmad* case.

In 1993, the Commission found no violation of a person's freedom to manifest their religion in the cases *Şenay Karaduman v. Turkey* and *Lamiye Bulut v. Turkey* regarding the stipulation that the heads of female students be uncovered on their student identity cards.[24] The Commission based its judgment on the fact that by agreeing to study at a secular university, the students had pledged to abide by the rules of the university. Therefore, there had been no violation of the Convention.

When in 1998 the ECtHR replaced the European Commission of Human Rights as a first instance mechanism, it handed down some significant judgments regarding this question. For instance, in 2001, the ECtHR made a judgment in the case of *Dahlab v. Switzerland*, where a primary school teacher, Lucia Dahlab, had been forbidden by the school authorities from wearing a headscarf.[25] The Swiss Federal court in 1997 found that the ban on Dahlab wearing a headscarf was reasonable, when it was considered that she taught very young pupils who could easily be influenced by their teacher. The ECtHR court rejected the application as manifestly ill-founded because the Court concluded that there was no discrimination on the grounds of sex.

In 2005, an application by Leyla Şahin, a Turkish medical student, went to the Grand Chamber of the ECtHR.[26] Following the introduction in 1998 of a ban on students in Turkey wearing headscarves in class or at examinations, the applicant left the University of İstanbul and continued her education in Austria. The Court noted that the ban existed when the applicant entered the university and that she should have known she would be prevented from going into class or examinations if she continued to wear a headscarf. The Court also stated that consideration should be given to the effect the wearing of a headscarf might have on those who did not wear headscarves. The Court, therefore, found that within the State's margin of appreciation, the measure could be seen as 'necessary in a democratic society' in accordance with paragraph 2 of article 9.

Two judgments in 2008, *Doğru v. France* and *Kervancı v. France* also addressed this issue.[27] The students named in the applications had enrolled in the first year of State middle schools. They had on several occasions donned headscarves when attending physical education and refused to take them off despite the insistence of teachers. The pupils had then been expelled from school—a decision subsequently ratified by local courts. The ECtHR judgment was that in both cases there had been no violation. The Court found that the decisions of the national authorities that the headscarf was inappropriate for physical education on health and safety grounds were not unreasonable. The Court drew attention to the fact the pupils had been expelled from school for breaking school rules, not on account of their religious beliefs.

The Court also handed down another judgment regarding France in 2008, in a case of a Sikh applicant by the name of Mann Singh.[28] The applicant claimed that his freedom to manifest his religious faith had been restricted by the French authorities insisting his photo on an application for a driving licence be taken without a turban. The Court judgment decided the freedom in question could be restricted on the grounds of 'public safety' and 'public order' mentioned in paragraph 2 of article 9 of the Convention and that therefore there had been no violation. The Court made reference to the principle of States' margin of appreciation in its judgment, but did not scrutinise the legitimacy or otherwise of the State's defence regarding establishing the identity of drivers and safeguarding against all manner of fraud.[29]

The Court also did not find violations of the Convention with a single judgment dealing with the following cases: *Aktaş v. France*, *Bayrak v. France*, *Gamaleddyn v. France*, *Ghazal v. France*, *J. Singh v. France* and *R. Singh v. France* cases in 2009.[30] These cases all involved the use of religious symbols by students on the first day of school when the four Muslim girls entered the class wearing headscarves and the two Sikh boys wore the small turban called a keski. The students were then expelled after refusing to remove the items of clothing. The ECtHR declared the applications inadmissible, saying that the interference in the freedom of the students to manifest their religion was based on laws that had the legitimate purpose of safeguarding the rights and freedoms of other people and protecting public order. The Court also stressed that States should be neutral towards religions and beliefs, and noted that the expulsion from school was not disproportionate, as the students involved had the opportunity to continue their education from home.

In 2010, the Court gave a judgment regarding the case brought by applicants from the Aczimendi Islamic brotherhood.[31] The applicants had been convicted in 1997 of contravening the law on headwear and on the wearing of religious clothing on the streets. The Court found that these persons did not pose a threat to public order, nor that there was any evidence of their aiming to convert any person passing their meetings by the use of coercion. The Court found the ban on the applicants' attire had been a violation of their right to manifest their religious beliefs. In other words, "the Court considered that the necessity for the disputed restriction had not been convincingly established by the Turkish Government, and held that the interference with the applicants' right of freedom to manifest their convictions had not been based on sufficient reasons".[32]

In 2011, the Grand Chamber handed down another judgment in the case of *Lautsi and others v. Italy*.[33] The problem was the display of a religious symbol by the State and not by an individual. However, it is still worth examining this case in detail to explore the approach of the ECtHR on the subject of freedom of religion. The children of the applicant went to a public school where the classrooms contained crucifixes. According to Ms Lautsi, this constituted a violation of the secular education she wished her children to receive. The school authorities refused to remove the crucifixes as requested by the applicant. Administrative courts also failed to resolve the matter. The ECtHR found a violation of article 9 in this case because the Court concluded that among the plurality of meanings the crucifix might have, the religious meaning was predominant.

However, the Grand Chamber took the opposite view, stating that it was within States' margin of appreciation as to whether there were religious symbols in classrooms. Nevertheless, it did stress that such decisions should not lead to indoctrination. The Grand Chamber noted that the widespread presence of crucifixes in State schools in Italy did not mean there was Christian indoctrination of pupils. The Court added that there was no evidence that the State was intolerant of students who had no religious belief or who held a different philosophy. The Court noted that Ms Lautsi had retained her right as a parent to enlighten and advise her children and to guide them on a path in line with her own philosophical convictions. The Grand Chamber also gave importance to the fact that in

Italian schools, pupils (and teachers) can freely wear religious symbols like the Islamic headscarf.[34] In conclusion the Grand Chamber ruled that article 2 of Protocol no. 1 had not been violated and that there was no need for a separate examination of the case under article 9 of the Convention.

The 2013 judgment of the Court regarding the use of religious symbols concerned the United Kingdom.[35] This case involved four people, the first of whom was a woman, Ms Eweida, who worked for British Airways. The applicant wanted to wear a crucifix, but this breached airline uniform policy rules. The applicant complained that she had been the victim of religious discrimination, but she had not been able to gain redress in domestic courts. Another applicant, Ms Chaplin, was a nurse who had been forbidden to wear a crucifix on duty on health and safety grounds. The final two applicants worked for Islington Council, Ms Ladele as a registrar and Mr McFarlane as a psychologist for a charity. Both applicants said that partnerships of same-sex couples conflicted with their religious beliefs. Hence, Ms Ladele stated that she would be unable to officiate in civil partnership ceremonies provided for by the 'Civil Partnership Act' of 2004.[36] Mr McFarlane stressed that he would be unable to provide psychological treatment to same-sex couples regarding sexuality.

In these cases, the ECtHR only found in favour of Ms Eweida, stating that the airline had not found a balance between the freedom and the restriction it had introduced. The Court emphasised the importance of equal treatment. In this case, Ms Eweida's right to manifest her religious belief had not been respected. The Court stated that as regards Ms Chaplin's application, rules on health and safety were important and that it was a legitimate aim to prohibit the use of ornaments. In the cases of Ms Ladele and Mr McFarlane, the Court also stated that the employer had aimed to secure the rights of others protected under the Convention and endeavoured to provide a service without discrimination.

Following this judgment, the Court has dealt with religious dress and/or symbol in several more cases. In 2015, in *Ebrahimian v. France* the Court found that there had been no violation of article 9.[37] In this case, the applicant, a hospital social worker, claimed her contract of employment had not been renewed on account of her refusal to stop wearing a Muslim veil. The applicant complained that the decision had been in breach of her right to the freedom to manifest her religion. The Court found that there had been no violation as the French authorities had acted within their margin of appreciation by finding it was not possible to reconcile the applicant's religious convictions and manifesting of them, and by opting to prioritise the State's duty of neutrality and impartiality. The Court emphasised that the authorities considered wearing a veil to be a manifestation of religion that was irreconcilable with public servants' duty of neutrality when discharging their functions. The French authorities had instructed the applicant to observe the principle of secularism enshrined in article 1 of the French Constitution and to behave in a manner based on that principle. The national courts had considered it necessary to defend the secular nature of the State and safeguard hospital patients from the risk of influence or partiality stemming from public servants asserting their right to freedom of conscience. The judgment in question had been based on the necessity of safeguarding the rights and freedoms of others—in other words, respect for everyone's religion or belief.

Hamidović v. Bosnia and Herzegovina in 2017 involved an applicant who, while a witness in a criminal trial, had been removed from the courtroom and convicted of contempt of court and fined for refusing to remove his skullcap.[38] In particular, he complained that the contempt of court charge had been disproportionate. The Court found that there had been a violation of article 9 and that there was no evidence that the applicant had acted in a disrespectful manner during the hearing. The Court found that his conviction for contempt of court solely based on his refusal to take off his skullcap, a religious symbol, could not be considered necessary in a democratic society and had violated his fundamental right to manifest his religion. The Court emphasised that this case was quite different from cases involving people wearing religious symbols and clothing in the work environment, particularly public officials. Public officials may have responsibilities such as impartiality, neutrality and discretion, meaning they cannot display religious symbols or wear religious clothing while on duty, which is not the case for private citizens such as the applicant.

The Court addressed the issue of wearing religious dress in public in two more cases on 11 July 2017: *Belcacemi and Oussar v. Belgium* and *Dakir v. Belgium*.[39] As these cases are similar, only one will be examined. *Dakir v. Belgium* focused on a by-law that three Belgian municipalities (Pepinster, Dison and Verviers) introduced in June 2008 that banned the wearing of clothing that conceals the face in public and related proceedings at the *Conseil d'État*. The Court found there had been no violation of articles 8 and 9 and no violation of article 14 of the Convention taken together with articles 8 and 9. The Court found in particular that the ban introduced in the Vesdre police area by the municipal by-law was proportionate to its purpose, that is, safeguarding the conditions of 'living together' as a component of protecting the rights and freedoms of others. Consequently, the Court found that the restriction at issue could be considered necessary in a democratic society and that the question as to whether people should be allowed to conceal the whole face behind a veil in Belgium was a choice for society. This was a similar situation to that in France. The Court did, however, conclude that article 6(1) of the Convention had been breached in this case. It found that the *Conseil d'État* decision to declare the applicant's application inadmissible because it was based only on article 113 bis of the by-law, without reference to article 113, had been too strict, as restricting the applicant's access to the *Conseil d'État* meant the balance between ensuring that the formal appeal procedure was observed, a legitimate concern, and the right of access to the courts, had not been struck. The Court emphasised that the applicant had made her case on the merits in a reasonable and structured way and was important.

In 2018, the Court concluded there had been a violation of article 9 in a judgment that was similar to the *Hamidović* judgment.[40] In this case, the applicant had been removed from a courtroom because she refused to take off her hijab. She claimed that this had violated her freedom to manifest her religion.

In most of the above cases, the Court noted that the essential point regarding the use of religious symbols is that they are necessary and convincing as regards the religious belief to which they belong.[41] In general, the Court allows a wide margin of appreciation to States in how they interpret the use of religious symbols in the public sphere. It pays attention to the principle of secularism and to whether there is a proportionality between the freedom enshrined in the first paragraph of article 9 and the reasons for limitations referred to in the second paragraph. When the Court determines the existence of legitimate aims such as health, safety and the provision of services without discrimination to others, it finds that there has been no violation of this article.

In conclusion, the ECtHR accepts the freedom of thought, conscience and religion as one of the most fundamental rights, maintaining a broad interpretation of article 18, in which this freedom is enshrined. It emphasises that individual freedoms cannot be restricted disproportionately in a democratic society unless absolutely necessary.[42] Hence, the ECtHR insistently makes clear in its judgments that States should be impartial towards all religions and beliefs and that they have a duty to protect people's freedom of thought, conscience and religion. It tells them not to forget that they have an obligation to encourage tolerance and multi-culturalism.[43] However, the ECtHR maintains a broad margin of appreciation for States as regards the manifesting of this freedom, finding restrictions introduced in accordance with paragraph 2 of article 9 to be proportional.

6.3 Turkey's Obligations

In this section, how courts in Turkey interpret this freedom and see whether there are similarities or differences will be examined. It will be essential while examining cases to look at the legal provisions in Turkey regarding the freedom in question. In this way, it will be possible to understand to what degree Turkey has fulfilled its obligations arising from international law. Additionally, these provisions and judicial interpretations of social and political events will enable us to understand different views on these topics. In other words, such an examination will portray the relationship between State and religion in Turkey and illustrate to what degree the State meets the criteria of impartiality towards religious belief.

In the Constitution of 1982 Turkey recognises the right to freedom of thought, conscience and religion in article 24. Therefore,[44]

> Everyone has the freedom of conscience, religious belief and conviction.
> Acts of worship, religious rites and ceremonies shall be conducted freely, as long as they do not violate the provisions of article 14.
> No one shall be compelled to worship, or to participate in religious rites and ceremonies, or to reveal religious beliefs and convictions, or be blamed or accused because of his religious beliefs and convictions.
> Religious and moral education and instruction shall be conducted under State supervision and control. Instruction in religious culture and morals shall be one of the compulsory lessons in the curricula of primary and secondary schools. Other religious education and instruction shall be subject to the individual's own desire, and in the case of minors, to the request of their legal representatives.
> No one shall be allowed to exploit or abuse religion or religious feelings, or things held sacred by religion, in any manner whatsoever, for the purpose of personal or political interest or influence, or for even partially basing the fundamental, social, economic, political, and legal order of the State on religious tenets.

Article 25 safeguards the freedom of thought and opinion thus:

Everyone has the freedom of thought and opinion.

No one shall be compelled to reveal his/her thoughts and opinions for any reason or purpose; nor shall anyone be blamed or accused because of his/her thoughts and opinions.

Article 10 of the Constitution also states that everyone is equal in the eyes of the law regardless of language, race, colour, gender, political opinion, philosophy, religion or sect, and that State organs and administrative courts have to act in accordance with the principle of equality.

Although in the Constitution, the freedom of thought, conscience and religion is safeguarded in clear terms, there are many provisions in law and regulation that impact negatively on this freedom: for instance, the Turkish Civil Code,[45] the Turkish Penal Code,[46] the Law on Rallies and Demonstrations,[47] the Law on Associations,[48] the Law on Foundations,[49] the Law on the Foundation of National Education,[50] the Law on the Private Education Establishments,[51] the Law on the Building Code,[52] the Law on the Closure of Dervish Convents and Tombs, the Abolition of the Office of Keeper of Tombs and the Abolition and Prohibition of Certain Titles[53] and the Law on the Prohibition of Wearing Certain Garments.[54][55]

It is a fact that these laws and the practices around them are not in harmony with the Constitution. Hence, there has been great controversy in Turkey as regards the subject of religious symbols and the question of the manifesting of religion or faith in the public sphere. The most blatant example of this has been the use of the headscarf.

It is necessary to explain why the headscarf should be a problem in a country where 95% of the population is considered to be Muslim.[56] The founders of the Republic of Turkey in 1923, first and foremost, Atatürk, insisted on the need for contemporary civilisation. The headscarf was seen "as a sign of ignorance, of fanaticism, of hatred to progress and civilisation".[57] Saktanber and Çorbacıoğlu summarised the development of social perceptions as regards the headscarf in the following words:

> [I]n the 1920s and 1930s…it was a question of civilization…the sign of western modernization while veiling was the sign of the rejected Ottoman past. In the 1940s and 1950s, it was associated with rural Turkey and singled out as a matter of underdevelopment, poverty, and tradition. In the 1960s and 1970s, it reappeared as an urban public issue…though the number of women who demanded to cover their heads in the public institutions was negligible. In the 1980s and 1990s, it became a matter of public con-

frontation with the state authorities as well as the secular sections of the civil society.[58]

In their judgments, the courts have dwelt in particular on the principle of secularism, which is enshrined in article 2 of the Constitution and is considered one of the six founding principles of the Republic. In 1998, the Constitutional Court stated in its decision on the Welfare Party *(Refah Partisi)* that secularism was one of the fundamental elements of society in the country.[59] The Council of State has also emphasised the principle of secularism in its judgments, presenting the headscarf as a negative example for the younger generation. For instance, in 2005, the Council of State said that a school headmistress who had been removed from her post after beginning to use a headscarf had a negative influence on children.[60]

The ban on the headscarf for public servants came onto the agenda after the military coup of 1980, as there was no such prohibition in Law no. 657 on Public Servants of 16 July 1965. The military coup of 12 September 1980 emphasised the principle of secularism as one of the reasons for its intervention, and Regulation no. 8/5105 on Dress of Personnel in State Institutions adopted on 16 July 1982 introduced detailed provisions pertaining to how men and women should dress. The following wording was introduced regarding women's attire:[61]

> Dresses, skirts and trousers shall be clean, straight, plain and ironed. Shoes and/or boots shall be plain, have normal heels and be polished. The head shall always be uncovered and the hair be tidy, combed or in a bun. Nails shall be trimmed. If for certain services special clothing is to be worn, this will be worn with the permission of the person in charge.
>
> Sleeveless blouses and those with very open collars and stretch jeans and similar garments shall not be worn. Skirts shall not be above the knee or with slashes. Sandals shall not be worn.

Only those personnel who wear uniforms were exempt from this regulation.[62] Hundreds of public servants resigned their posts on account of the headscarf ban. For instance, Dr Koru was removed from her post at the University of the Aegean in 1984 on account of her wearing a headscarf. The Court decided that the headscarf was not included in the definition of freedom of religion and that this was not possible in a secular state structure.[63] There were many such decisions, particularly in the 28 February period, with many public servants being affected.[64] The Women's Rights Organisation Against Discrimination submitted a report to the

Organization for Security and Co-Operation in Europe (OSCE) which contained the following:

> Between 1998 and 2002 about five thousand civil servants were dismissed from their positions and about ten thousand of them were forced to resign because they wore the headscarf.[65]

During this period, the army and some sections of society, the media and politicians endeavoured to legitimise these bans within the framework of the principle of secularism. One of the most controversial incidents involved Merve Kavakçı, who was elected as a Member of Parliament (MP) in 1999. She was an MP from Virtue Party (*Fazilet Partisi*).[66] When Ms Kavakçı wanted to swear the oath of allegiance in the Turkish Parliament wearing a headscarf, she encountered serious opposition from some deputies.[67] The ECtHR declined to examine the case under article 9 of the Convention, finding a violation of article 3 of Protocol no. 1 because of her expulsion from the Turkish Parliament.[68] The Court pointed out that it was not clear why the applicant had been prosecuted, as regards the principle of proportionality.[69] During this period, Sevgi Kurtulmuş, a lecturer at the University of İstanbul, made an application to the ECtHR, which was declared inadmissible.[70]

The Regulation Concerning the Dress of Personnel Employed in Public Institutions referred to above, which is the source of the headscarf ban for public servants, was revised on 4 October 2013 by change no. 2013/5443. The new wording is as follows:

> Sleeveless blouses and those with very open collars and stretch jeans and similar garments shall not be worn. Skirts shall not be above the knee or with slashes. Sandals shall not be worn.[71]

This change ended the ban on the headscarf amongst public servants with the exception of the following sectors: police, justice and military.[72] It should be noted that the restrictions on the mentioned-exempted sectors were subsequently lifted.[73]

In October 2013, four MPs wore headscarves in the Turkish Parliament.[74] The Council of State even reviewed past judgments, stating that when lawyers registered with Bar associations, they would be able to submit photos with headscarves.[75] Changes were also made to the regulation applying to male public servants, the new wording being as follows:

> Clothes shall be clean, straight, plain and ironed. Shoes shall be clean and polished. Sandals shall not be worn. The head shall always be uncovered within the premises and at the place of duty. Earrings shall not be worn. Hair shall not cover the ear and not be longer than the collar, and shall be clean and combed. Personnel shall shave on a daily basis and beards shall not be grown. Moustaches shall be left natural, with the length not to be longer than the upper lip. Ties shall be worn. Sweaters or other garments that cover the tie may not be worn. If necessary, for the service provided, a single type of clothing shall be worn. People shall not walk around the premises without a shirt, tie or socks.[76]

While the ban on the headscarf for women has now been abolished, for male public servants there are still existing bans. For instance, a Jewish man cannot wear a kippah (brimless cap), and there is no possibility of a person growing a beard or not wearing a tie on account of their religious beliefs.

The above regulations on dress and appearance form the basis of prohibitions on the use of religious symbols by public servants. However, the question of headscarves for university students was also prominent on the agenda for a long period, and it will be useful to take a look at the legal provisions in this area. In fact, while there is no provision for university students in the Regulation governing Discipline in Higher Education, in 1988 a provision was added to the supplementary article 16 of the Law on Higher Education, as follows:

> In institutions of higher education, it is compulsory to wear contemporary attire in classrooms, laboratories, clinics, polyclinics and corridors. [Students] are free to cover their neck and hair with a scarf or turban due to religious beliefs.[77]

The intention of this change was to make it possible to wear a headscarf. However, a case was initiated by the President at the Constitutional Court, which found the provision to be in violation of the Constitution, making reference to the principle of a secular state. As a result, the Court abolished this article.[78]

With this judgment, the Constitutional Court stood behind its previous judgments, again finding the headscarf violated the principle of secularism enshrined in the Constitution. However, the difference in this judgment is that the headscarf is referred to as 'a matter of personal preference', rather than as 'in contravention of contemporary life' as in previous judgments. The Court recognises the possibility that different ways of life may constitute an imposition on others, pointing out that this right may be restricted legitimately in accordance with paragraph 2 of article 9 of the Convention.[79] Hence, the Court actually handed down this judgment taking into consideration the judgments of the ECtHR. For instance, the reference made by the ECtHR to the margin of appreciation of States in the *Leyla Şahin* case and its consideration of the principle of secularism is important. However, in recent judgments of the ECtHR in cases such as *Eweida* and others it is significant that the Court has stressed the need for a balance between the interests of society and the individual. Hence, it is important that the Constitutional Court in Turkey has taken this into consideration when reaching judgments.[80] In other words, when the right to use religious symbols is granted to people within the scope of the freedom of thought, conscience and religion, these symbols should not be used to constitute an imposition on others.[81]

After a long period in Turkey when many students had to cut short their education on account of the restriction on the headscarf, in 2011, an amnesty was declared that enabled students to return to their universities.[82] Since regulations are the source of provisions outlining the dress and appearance of public servants and students in Turkey, a change in these regulations was sufficient to allow the wearing of headscarves in universities. However, this means that a change in the political atmosphere in the country could lead to the headscarf ban being reintroduced merely by a change in the regulations. It may thus be stated that since it is much more difficult to change the laws and the Constitution, it is necessary that such a crucial freedom as the use of religious symbols be safeguarded by the Constitution or at least by laws.

Mention has been made above of the problems experienced in the past by public servants and students as regards the use of the headscarf. However, it should not be forgotten that parents of students have also had problems. In 2002 at the Atatürk University in Erzurum, parents of students were not allowed to attend a graduation ceremony on account of wearing the headscarf. Only after donning wigs were they allowed to attend.[83] In 2003, a lawyer by the name of Hatice Hasdemir Şahin was not allowed to enter a court wearing a headscarf.[84] The Council of State even declared in a judgment regarding a trainee lawyer that in her private life outside court, the wearing of a headscarf did not accord with the secular state structure.[85] Those who supported the right to wear headscarves were also punished, with the Dean of the Faculty of Medicine at the Yüzüncü

Yıl University, Prof. Dursun Odabaş, being removed from his post in 1998.[86]

It should be noted that following the military coup of 1980, every single religious or ideological activity was banned and in the oppressive environment thus created the discourse of 'secular state' was used constantly by the authorities to legitimise these bans. However, with the change in the political conjuncture in Turkey and the recent changes to legal provisions, there is no longer any problem regarding the use of the headscarf in the public sphere. However, the manifesting of religion or belief in the public sphere cannot be confined solely to an examination of the headscarf issue, and it is therefore important to look at the situation regarding the use of other religious symbols. For instance, restrictions on dress representing religious status or position contained in Law no. 2596 on the Pertaining to Certain Garments that May Not be Worn remains in force.[87] This law prohibits a minister of any religion from wearing clothes that represent their position outside the place of worship. However, a decision of the Council of Ministers allows a representative of certain religious groups to wear attire representing their post in public spaces.[88]

The ECtHR handed down a judgment regarding this issue in the case of *Ahmet Arslan and others v. Turkey*.[89] In this case, members of the Aczimendi Islamic order were prosecuted for wearing attire in public in accordance with their religious beliefs. The Court found that the conviction violated article 9 of the Convention. In spite of this judgment, the State has yet to implement the required legal reform to prevent a recurrence of such violations.[90]

In fact, even with the existing Constitution, which is the product of a military coup, this freedom may be interpreted in accordance with fundamental rights and freedoms. However, as mentioned above, it appears that there is a distinct clash between the Constitution, laws and practical implementation. Unfortunately, most of the laws in Turkey are not appropriate to either the Constitution or international legal norms. In such situations, paragraph 5 of article 90 of the Constitution makes it clear that in the event of conflict between international agreements and domestic law, international agreements will be adhered to.

This article makes it clear that Turkey has an obligation to safeguard the freedom of thought, conscience and religion as it is protected in international law. The Committee of Ministers of the Council of Europe also stated that in accordance with articles 46 of the ECHR and 90(5) of the Constitution, both the ECHR and the judgments of the ECtHR should be directly applied in Turkish law.[91] However, as noted by the Turkish former ECtHR judge, Işıl Karataş, one of the reasons for Turkey's continuing problem lies in the judicial pronouncements of Turkish judges who persistently fail to comply with ECtHR decisions.[92] Of course, this issue is not solely about the failure of the judiciary to act in harmony with ECtHR judgments or more generally in accordance with international norms. Executive and legislative authorities must fulfil their obligations arising from international law around this issue.

In conclusion, while the subject of the use of religious symbols was concentrated around headscarves for a long time, as mentioned above, and as permission has now been given for its use in the public sphere, there remain problems as regards the use of other religious symbols. Beliefs and religions apart from the dominant Sunni Muslim faith suffer blatant discrimination. In order for these problems to be resolved, it is essential that the State authorities reinterpret concepts such as fundamental rights and freedoms according to current circumstances. It is also necessary for the negative effects of the 1980 coup to be immediately removed from all areas of life. This could begin with a new Constitution accompanied by legal reforms, leading in the long term to a change in mentality.

6.4 Conclusion

In Turkey, the use of religious symbols, in particular the headscarf, was on the agenda for a long time and still reappears from time to time. The reason for this was that for a long period the headscarf was seen as an obstacle to civilisation. This view is still held by certain sections of society. Therefore, court judgments constantly emphasised the principle of secularism. Of course, while the issue of the headscarf is important, the question of religious symbols cannot be confined solely to this one issue. Legal reform in 2013 allowed the use of the headscarf in the public sphere. Many public servants were thus able to return to their posts. An amnesty declared in 2011 permitted university students who had been unable to continue their education to return to their studies. Although these legal reforms have resolved to some degree the issue of the headscarf, restrictions remain on the manifestation of religion or belief in the public sphere. While there has been a relaxation regarding public servants wearing the headscarf or having permission to attend Friday prayers, discrimination still exists for those who are not adherents of the Sunni Muslim faith. Due to this discriminative approach, many people suffer discrimination on account of their religion or belief and have to terminate their work or education on account of this.

In Turkey, where there are problems regarding the separation of powers and a lack of written norms, it does not appear possible for this freedom to be entirely safeguarded. It is therefore important that reforms being made regarding the use of religious symbols, in particular around the headscarf issue, should be guaranteed by article 24 of the Turkish Constitution and relevant laws, not by regulations, as regulations are subordinate to the Constitution and laws. If political conditions were to change in Turkey in the future, there is no guarantee that restrictions on the use of religious symbols, first and foremost the headscarf, would not be reintroduced. It is essential that the use of religious symbols be given stronger legal guarantees and that these regulations also protect religions and beliefs other than the dominant Sunni belief from discrimination.

NOTES

1. *Kokkinakis v. Greece*, 25 May 1993, No. 14307/88, para. 31.
2. According to the ECHR, there are four particular forms of manifestation: worship, teaching, practice and observance. See M. D. Evans, *Manual on the Wearing of Religious Symbols in Public Areas* (Strasbourg: Council of Europe, 2009), p. 12.
3. *Mustafa Ünsal*, Council of State 5. Section, 17 December 1999, E. 1999/4212, K. 1999/4325; *Kevser Sönmez*, Sakarya 2. Administrative Court, 26 December 2001, E. 2001/14, K. 2001/2854.
4. D. Cindoğlu, *Başörtüsü Yasağı ve Ayrımcılık: Uzman Meslek Sahibi Başörtülü Kadınlar* (İstanbul, Türkiye Ekonomik ve Sosyal Etütler Vakfı, 2010), pp. 5, 7; M. Yıldırım, 'Turkish Workplace: The Approach of the Turkish Judiciary', in K. Alidadi, M.-C. Foblets & J. Vrielink (eds.), *A Test of Faith? Religious Diversity and Accommodation in the European* Workplace (Surrey: Routledge, 2012), pp. 183–204.
5. K. Boyle, 'Freedom of Conscience, Pluralism and Tolerance: Freedom of Conscience in International Law', in Council of Europe, *Freedom of Conscience* (Strasbourg: Council of Europe Press, 1993), p. 42; R. Reilly, 'Conscience, Citizenship, and Global Responsibilities', 23 *Buddhist-Christian Studies* (2003), pp. 117–131; K. J. Partsch, 'Freedom of Conscience and Expression, and Political Freedoms', in L. Henkin (ed.), *The International Bill of Rights* (New York: Columbia University Press, 1981), p. 213.

6. B. G. Tahzib, *Freedom of Religion or Belief Ensuring Effective International Legal Protection* (Leiden: Martinus Nijhoff Publishers, 1996), pp. 72, 73.
7. Article 29 states: "1. Everyone has duties to the community in which alone the free and full development of his personality is possible; 2. In the exercise of his rights and freedoms, everyone shall be subject only to such limitations as are determined by law solely for the purpose of securing due recognition and respect for the rights and freedoms of others and of meeting the just requirements of morality, public order and the general welfare in a democratic society; 3. These rights and freedoms may in no case be exercised contrary to the purposes and principles of the United Nations."

    Article 30 states: "Nothing in this Declaration may be interpreted as implying for any State, group or person any right to engage in any activity or to perform any act aimed at the destruction of any of the rights and freedoms set forth herein."
8. J. Murdock, *Freedom of Thought, Conscience and Religion – A Guide to the Implementation of Article 9 of the European Convention on Human Rights* (Strasbourg: Council of Europe, 2007), p. 31. Also see M. T. Parker, 'The Freedom to Manifest Religious Belief: An Analysis of the Necessity Clauses of the ICCPR and the ECHR', 17 *Duke Journal of Comparative & International Law* (2006), pp. 91–130; Evans, *supra note* 2, pp. 17–21.
9. See, for example, *Chappell v. United Kingdom*, 1987-53 Eur. Comm'n H. R. 247; *X v. the Netherlands*, 1962- 5 Y. B. Eur. Conv. on H. R. 284.
10. See, for example, *X v. Sweden*, 1984-5 Eur. Ct. H.R. 297; *X v. the Federal Republic of Germany*, 1987-11 Eur. Comm'n H.R.102.
11. See, for example, *X v. United Kingdom*, 1976- 5 Eur. Comm'n H.R. 100.
12. See, for example, *Kokkinakis v. Greece*, *supra note* 1; *Larissis and others v. Greece*, 1998-V Eur. CT. H. R. 363.
13. See, for example, *Pentidis and others v. Greece*, 1996-III Eur. Comm'n H.R. 4 (friendly settlement); *Kokkinakis v. Greece*, *supra note* 1, para. 47; *Manoussakis and others v. Greece*, 1996 Eur. Ct. H. R. 41, para 44.
14. *Handyside v. United Kingdom*, 1976 Eur. Ct. H. R. 5, paras. 49–50.
15. Article 15 states: "In time of war or other public emergency threatening the life of the nation any High Contracting Party may take measures derogating from its obligations under this Convention to the extent strictly required by the exigencies of the situation, provided that such measures are not inconsistent with its other obligations under international law."
16. Helsinki Final Act is the final act of the 1st Conference on Security and Cooperation in Europe (CSCE) Summit of Heads of State or Government. The CSCE started drafting in Helsinki on 3 July 1973 and worked between 18 September 1973 and 21 July 1975 in Geneva, concluding in Helsinki on 1 August 1975 with representatives of the following countries: Austria, Belgium, Bulgaria, Canada, Cyprus, Czechoslovakia, Denmark, Finland,

France, The Democratic Republic of Germany, the Federal Republic of Germany, Greece, the Vatican City State, Hungary, Iceland, Ireland, Italy, Lichtenstein, Luxemburg, Malta, Monaco, The Netherlands, Norway, Poland, Portugal, Romania, the United Kingdom (UK), San Marino, Spain, Sweden, Switzerland, Turkey, the Union of Soviet Socialist Republics (USSR), the United States of America (USA) and Yugoslavia.

17. Proclaimed by resolution no. 36/55 of the General Assembly of the United Nations on 25 November 1981.
18. Human Rights Commission, *19 April 2005*, E/CN.4/RES/2005/40, *art. 4(b)*.
19. Evans, *supra note* 2, pp. 62–68.
20. Isabelle Rorive, 'Religious Symbols in the Public Space: In Search of a European Answer', 30 *Cardozo Law Review* (2009), pp. 2676–2787. Also see European Court of Human Rights, (July 2014), 'Factsheet: Religious symbols and clothing', http://www.echr.coe.int/Documents/FS_Religious_Symbols_ENG.pdf, accessed 21 September 2020.
21. Eleventh Protocol opened up for signatures on 11 May 1994 and came into force on 1 November 1998.
22. *Ahmad v. United Kingdom*, 1981- 4 Eur. Comm'n H. R. 126.
23. *Stedman v. United Kingdom*, 1997- 23 Eur. Comm'n H. R. 104.
24. *Karaduman v. Turkey*, 1993-74 Eur. Comm'n H. R. 93; *Lamiye Bulut v. Turkey*, 1993- 74 Eur. Comm'n H.R. 93.
25. *Dahlab v. Switzerland*, 2001-V Eur. Ct. H. R. 899.
26. *Leyla Şahin v. Turkey (Grand Chamber)*, 2005-XI Eur. Ct. H. R. 819.
27. *Doğru v. France and Kervancı v. France*, 2008-49 Eur. Ct. H. R. 179.
28. *Mann Singh v. France*, No. 24479/07, 2008 Eur. Ct. H. R (unpublished).
29. S. E. Berry, (2013), 'Freedom of Religion and Religious Symbols: Same Right – Different Interpretation', *Blog of the European Journal of International Law*, http://www.ejiltalk.org/freedom-of-religion-and-religious-symbols-same-right-different-interpretation/, accessed 21 September 2020.
30. *Aktas v. France*, No. 43563/08, *Bayrak v. France*, No. 14308/08, *Gamaleddyn v. France*, No. 18527/08, *Ghazal v. France*, No. 29134/08, *J. Singh v. France*, No. 25463/08 and *R. Singh v. France*, No. 27561/08, 2009 Eur. Ct. H. R. 1142.
31. *Ahmet Arslan and others v. Turkey*, 23 February 2010, No. 41135/98.
32. Ibid., para. 52.
33. *Lautsi and others v. Italy (GC)*, 18 March 2011, No. 30814/06.
34. Ibid., para. 74.
35. *Eweida and others v. United Kingdom*, 15 January 2013, Nos. 48420/10, 59842/10, 51671/10 and 36516/10.
36. Civil Partnership Act, 2004.

37. *Ebrahimian v. France*, 26 November 2015, No. 64846/11.
38. *Hamidović v. Bosnia and Herzegovina*, 5 December 2017, No. 57792/15.
39. *Belcacemi and Oussar v. Belgium*, 11 July 2017, No. 37798/13; *Dakir v. Belgium*, 11 July 2017, No. 4619/12.
40. *Lachiri v. Belgium*, 18 September 2018, No. 3413/09.
41. H. Kurt, 'İnanç Özgürlüğü Bağlamında Dini Sembollerin Kullanımının Mukayeseli Hukuk Bakımından Değerlendirilmesi', 12 *Erzincan Üniversitesi Hukuk Fakültesi Dergisi* (2013), p. 228.
42. S. O. Chaib, (2013), 'Freedom of Religion in Public Schools: Strasbourg Court v. UN Human Rights Committee', http://strasbourgobservers.com/2013/02/14/freedom-of-religion-in-public-schools-strasbourg-court-v-un-human-rights-committee/, accessed 21 September 2020.
43. Evans, *supra note* 2, pp. 49–50.
44. 1982 Constitution of Republic of Turkey, published in Official Gazette dated 7 November 1982 (No. 2709), and dated 9 November 1982 (No. 17863).
45. Turkish Civil Code, Pub. L. No. 4721 (2001).
46. Turkish Penal Code, Pub. L. No. 5237 (2004).
47. Law on Rallies and Demonstrations, Pub. L. No. 2911 (1983).
48. Law on Associations, Pub. L. No. 5253 (2004).
49. Law on Foundations, Pub. L. No. 573 (2008).
50. Law on the Foundation of National Education, Pub. L. No. 1739 (1973).
51. Law on the Private Education Establishments, Pub. L. No. 5580 (2007).
52. Law on the Building Code, Pub. L. No. 3194 (1985).
53. Law on the Closure of Dervish Convents and Tombs, the Abolition of the Office of Keeper of Tombs and the Abolition and Prohibition of Certain Titles, Pub. L. No. 677 (1925).
54. Law on the Prohibition of Wearing Certain Garments, Pub. L. No. 2879 (1934).
55. NHC: İÖG, (2014), 'Monitoring Report on the Right to Freedom of Religion or Belief in Turkey July 2013–June 2014', p. 9, http://inancozgurlugugirisimi.org/wp-content/uploads/2014/10/NHC-%C4%B0%C3%96G-T%C3%BCrkiyede-%C4%B0nan%C3%A7-%C3%96zg%C3%BCrl%C3%BC%C4%9F%C3%BC-Hakk%C4%B1n%C4%B1-%C4%B0zleme-Raporu.pdf, accessed 21 September 2020.
56. R. Bottoni, 'Legal, Political and Social Obstacles for Headscarved Women Working at State Institutions in Turkey', 8 *Religion and Human Rights: An International Journal* (2013), p. 184.
57. Bottoni, *supra note* 56, p. 184.
58. A. Saktanber and G. Çorbacıoğlu, 'Veiling and Headscarf-Skepticism in Turkey', 15 *Social Politics* (2008), p. 519.

59. Bottoni, *supra note* 56, p. 184, footnote 73. Please note that Refah Party was an Islamist political party established in 1983 in Turkey.
60. Ibid., p. 190, footnote 29.
61. Regulation Concerning the Dress of Personnel Employed in Public Institutions, Pub. L. No. 8/5105 (1982), art. 5(a).
62. Ibid., art. 6.
63. R. Bottoni, 'The Headscarf Issue at State Institutions in Turkey: From the Kemalist Age to Recent Developments', in Ö. H. Çınar & M. Yıldırım (eds.), *Freedom of Religion and Belief in Turkey* (Newcastle upon Tyne: Cambridge Scholars, 2014), pp. 123–124.
64. Bottoni, *supra note* 63, p. 124. Also see A. A. Ahmad Na'Im, *Islam and the Secular State: Negotiating the Future of Shari'a* (Harvard: Harvard University Press, 2008), p. 208.
65. Women's Rights Organisation Against Discrimination (AKDER), (2008), *A Statistical Examination of the Condition of Women in Turkey and the Impact of the Headscarf Ban on Turkey's Gender Equality Ranking*, p. 7, www.osce.org/odihr/39070, accessed 21 September 2020.
66. Fazilet Party was an Islamist political party established in 1998 in Turkey.
67. AKDER, *supra note* 65, p. 11.
68. *Kavakçı v. Turkey*, 2007 Eur. Ct. H. R.
69. Ibid., para. 44.
70. *Kurtulmuş v. Turkey*, 2006 Eur. Ct. H. R. 2.
71. Amendment to the Regulation Concerning the Dress of Personnel Employed in Public Institutions was accepted by the Ministry of Cabinet on 4 October 2013, Decision no. 2013/5443. It was published in the Official Gazette dated 8 October 2013 (No. 28789).
72. The latest version of Article 5(c) of the Regulation Concerning the Dress of Personnel Employed in Public Institutions is as follows: "However, if there is any specific work uniform for the described services, these uniforms must be used with the permission of the organisation manager during this service."

    Article 6 states: "The members of the police force, judges, public prosecutors, and the personnel of the Turkish Armed Forces are subject to the systematic rules described by the Regulation of their establishment and organisation."
73. 'TSK'da Başörtüsü Yasağı Kalktı', *DW*, 22 February 2017, https://www.dw.com/tr/tskda-ba%C5%9F%C3%B6rt%C3%BCs%C3%BC-yasa%C4%9F%C4%B1-kalkt%C4%B1/a-37665858, accessed 21 September 2020.
74. 'Türbanlı Vekiller Mecliste', *Milliyet*, 31 October 2013, http://www.milliyet.com.tr/ilk-turbanli-vekil-geldi/siyaset/detay/1785020/default.htm, accessed 21 September 2020.

75. 'Turkish Court Lifts Headscarf Ban for Attorneys', *Hürriyet*, 11 November 2013, http://www.hurriyetdailynews.com/turkish-court-lifts-headscarf-ban-for-attorneys.aspx?pageID=238&nID=57762&NewsCatID=339, accessed 21 September 2020.
76. Regulation Concerning the Dress of Personnel Employed in Public Institutions, art. 5(b).
77. This article was added on 10 December 1988, Law no. 3511, article 2. Also see Law on Higher Education, Law no. 2547, adopted 4 November 1981, Official gazette dated 6 November 1981 (No. 17506).
78. *Kenan Evren*, Constitutional Court, 7 March 1989, E. 1989/1, K. 1989/12. Also see Kurt, *supra note* 41, p. 215.
79. Kurt, *supra note* 41, p. 216.
80. *Eweida and others v. United Kingdom*, *supra note* 35, para. 84.
81. *Larissis and others v. Greece*, *supra note* 12. Also see A. R. Güder, 'Kamu Görevlilerinin Dini Sembol Taşıyabilmesinin Sınırları: Eski Bir Tartışma ve Yeni Hukuki Paradigmalar', 111 *Türkiye Barolar Birliği Dergisi* (2014), p. 476; Evans, *supra* note 2, pp. 27, 67, 97, 104–105.
82. Law on Restructuring of Some Receivables and Social Security/General Health, Pub. L. No. 6111 (2011), art. 171, 172 & 173.
83. A. Ü. Ekinci, (2009), 'Dini Semboller – Başörtüsü İkilemi ve Uluslararası İnsan Hakları Hukuku', http://www.turkhukuksitesi.com/makale_984.htm, accessed 21 September 2020.
84. Ekinci, *supra note* 83, footnote no. 95.
85. Turkish Bar Association, Council of State 8. Section, 2 March 1994, E. 1993/843, K. 1994/686. Also see AKDER, *supra note* 65, p. 7, footnote no. 25.
86. MazlumDer, (2001), 'YÖK'ün İnsan Hakları İhlalleri Raporu', http://www.mazlumder.org/tr/main/yayinlar/yurt-ici-raporlar/3/yok-un-insan-haklari-ihlalleri-raporu-ankara-/1010, accessed 21 September 2020; Human Rights Watch, (2004), 'Memorandum to the Turkish Government on Human Rights Watch's Concerns with Regard to Academic Freedom in Higher Education, and Access to Higher Education for Women who Wear the Headscarf', pp. 31–32, https://www.hrw.org/sites/default/files/related_material/headscarf_memo.pdf, accessed 21 September 2020.
87. Law on the Pertaining to Certain Garments that May Not be Worn, Pub. L. No. 2596 (1934).
88. NHC: İÖG, *supra note* 55, p. 26.
89. *Ahmet Arslan and others v. Turkey*, *supra note* 31.
90. NHC: İÖG, *supra note* 55, p. 26.
91. The Committee of Ministers approached this issue at its meetings on 5 December 2006, 13 February 2007, 3 April 2007, 5 June 2007, 15 October 2007, 3 December 2007, 4 March 2008, 18 September 2008, 19

March 2009, 8 June 2011 and 14 September 2011. At their meeting on 19 March 2009, the Committee of Ministers came to a decision which "STRONGLY URGES the Turkish authorities to take without further delay all necessary measures to put an end to the violation of the applicant's rights under the Convention and to make the legislative changes necessary to prevent similar violations of the Convention". It went on to say that the Committee of Ministers will "continue examining the implementation of the present judgment at each human rights meeting until the necessary urgent measures are adopted" (Council of Europe, Committee of Ministers, 19 March 2009, Interim Resolution CM/ResDH(2009)45).

92. An interview with Işıl Karataş, 'Karakaş: "Vicdani ret hakkı mutlaka tanınmalı"', *EurActiv*, 29 November 2011, http://www.euractiv.com.tr/ab-ve-turkiye/article/karakas-vicdani-ret-hakki-mutlaka-taninmali-022703, accessed 21 September 2020.

Index[1]

A
Aczimendi, 122, 132
Agnostics, 1, 11, 61, 70
Ahmad v. United Kingdom, 120
Ahmet Arslan and others v. Turkey, 132
Ahtamar church, 102
Aktaş v. France, 121
Alevis, 4, 62, 64, 82, 91, 93, 94, 97, 98, 100, 103, 104, 106
  Alevi workshops, 64, 70
Alexandridis v. Greece, 16
Alienating the public from military service, 43
Altınay, Ayşe Gül, 44, 51n35, 53n50, 53n53, 53n54, 53n55
Altınkaynak and others v. Turkey, 102
Altıparmak, Kerem, 33n78, 69, 70
Angelini v. Sweden, 60
Anti-terror Law, 43
Appeal, right to, 39, 125
Armenian Orthodox Christians
Armenian Apostolic Church, 94, 105
Armenian Apostolic Church's Holy Cross Seminary, 105
Article 10, of Charter of Fundamental Rights of the European Union (Charter), 36, 48n4
Article 10, of Turkish Constitution 1982, 95
Article 101, of Turkish Civil Code, 92, 106
Article 11, of ECHR, 89–91, 102
Article 12(1), of Ibero-American Convention on Young People's Rights, 36
Article 12, of State Education Act, 29n1, 48n4, 69
Article 13, of Turkish Constitution 1982, 70
Article 14, of ECHR, 61
Article 14, of Turkish Constitution 1982, 95

---

[1] Note: Page numbers followed by 'n' refer to notes.

© The Author(s), under exclusive license to Springer Nature Switzerland AG 2021
Ö. H. Çınar, *Freedom of Religion and Belief in Turkey*,
https://doi.org/10.1007/978-3-030-70077-5

141

142 INDEX

Article 14, of UN Convention on the Rights of the Child, 58
Article 15, of ECHR, 12
Article 15, of Turkish Constitution 1982, 12
Article 17, of Turkish Constitution 1982, 45
Article 174, of Turkish Constitution 1982, 95, 96
Article 18, of Building Law, 98
Article 18, of ICCPR, 8–11, 29n1, 37, 38, 58, 59, 83, 117
Article 18, of UDHR, 8–11, 36, 38, 117
Article 19(6), of Constitution of Portugal, 12
Article 19, of Turkish Constitution 1961, 66, 67
Article 2, of Turkish Constitution 1982, 68, 95
Article 2, protocol 1 of the ECHR, 9, 15, 21, 24, 30n21, 62, 63, 68, 95, 123, 128
Article 20, of Turkish Constitution 1982, 45
Article 21, of the Charter, 12
Article 22, of the Charter, 12
Article 233(1), of Constitution of Poland, 12
Article 24, of Turkish Constitution 1982, 24, 26, 28, 42, 61, 64, 67–72, 92, 95, 105, 126, 134
Article 25, of State Education Act, 71
Article 25, of Turkish Constitution 1982, 28
Article 26(3), of UDHR, 58
Article 29, of UDHR, 135n7
Article 30, of UDHR, 135n7
Article 318, of the Turkish Penal Code, 43, 53n45
Article 4(3), of ECHR, 38
Article 4, of ICCPR, 37, 49n8, 52n42
Article 44, of Building Law, 98
Article 45, of [Turkish] Military Penal Code, 42
Article 46, of ECHR, 63, 75n23
Article 6, of Declaration on the Elimination of All Forms of Intolerance and of Discrimination Based on Religion or Belief, 18, 27, 91, 118, 138n72
Article 7, of Helsinki Final Act, 18, 97, 118
Article 72, of Turkish Constitution 1982, 42
Article 8(3)(c)(ii), of ICCPR, 38, 50n13
Article 8, of ECHR, 29n1, 54n62
Article 9, of ECHR, 2, 3, 11–14, 16–18, 20, 29n1, 38–40, 50n15, 52n40, 61, 63, 70, 71, 83, 85–91, 98, 103, 107, 117, 120–126, 129, 131, 132
Article 90(5), of Turkish Constitution 1982, 28, 73, 106, 132
Atatürk, 44, 68, 131
Ateşyan, Aram, 104
Atheists, 1, 11, 13, 14, 70, 107n1

B

Baháʾí/Baháʾís, 23, 82, 94, 107n1
Bal, Mehmet, 46, 47n3, 55n64
Bayatyan v Armenia, 40, 49n12
Bayrak v. France, 121
Bektaşi, 17
Belcacemi and Oussar v. Belgium, 124
Believers, 2, 12, 90
Bessarabie Metropolitan Church and others v Moldova, 90
Birth certificates, 7
Board of Education and Discipline, 68
Boyle, Kevin, 9, 10, 29n5, 48n7, 49n12
Brunson, Andrew, 104

C

Campbell and Cosans v. the United Kingdom, 69
Çankaya Cemevi Yaptırma Derneği (Association), 100
Catholic, 13, 23, 94, 102, 107n1
Çelik, Furkan, 43
Çelik, Ömer, 69
Cem houses (cemevi), 100
CEM Vakfı (the Foundation for Republican Education and Culture), 87, 88, 99–101
Christian, 65, 68, 70, 98, 105, 116, 120, 122
Civil death, 41
Closure of Dervish Convents and Tombs, the Abolition of the Office of Keeper of Tombs and the Abolition and Prohibition of Certain Titles, 96, 103, 127
Çolak, Yılmaz, 22, 32n60
Commission on Human Rights, 5n1, 119
Committee of Ministers, 39, 50n21, 59, 60, 63, 64, 73, 75–76n23, 100, 106, 132, 139–140n91
Compulsory military service, 38
Compulsory religious education, 3, 4, 57–74
Conscience, freedom of, 1, 2, 8–13, 16, 19, 20, 23, 25, 26, 28, 29n4, 29n5, 36–40, 42, 46, 48n6, 48n7, 50n15, 58, 66, 70, 73, 74, 83, 95, 115–119, 124–127, 131, 132
Conscientious objection, 3, 12, 35–43, 46, 47n1, 47n2, 48n4, 48n5, 49n12, 50n13, 51n30
Conscientious Objection Association, 43
Conscientious objectors, 35–46, 53n57
homosexual conscientious objectors, 45

Conscription, 39, 46
Constitutional Court of Turkey, 20, 131
Çorbacıoğlu, Gül, 127
Çorlu Military Hospital Medical Council, 46
Council of Europe, 29n5, 30n18, 31n47, 39, 47n2, 48–49n7, 59, 63, 82, 92, 94, 119, 132, 140n91
Council of State, 61, 71–74, 128, 129, 131
Court of Cassation, 17, 99, 100
Cumhuriyetçi Eğitim ve Kültür Merkezi Vakfı v. Turkey, 87, 98

D

Dahlab v. Switzerland, 120
Dakir v. Belgium, 124
Democratic society, 1, 11, 13, 41, 50n15, 54n62, 70, 84, 87, 89, 90, 103, 115, 117, 119, 121, 124, 125, 135n7
Desertion (firar), 42
Dimitras and others v. Greece, 16
Dimitrova v. Bulgaria, 88
Directorate of Religious Affairs (*Diyanet İşleri Başkanlığı-Diyanet*), 3, 17
Disciplinary proceedings, 43
Discrimination, 5n1, 8, 9, 12–15, 24, 25, 27, 28, 29n2, 36, 37, 39, 47n2, 49n8, 88, 95, 97, 106, 118–120, 123, 125, 133, 134
Disobedience, 42
Diyarbakır Metropolitan Municipality, 105
Doğru v. France, 121
Domestic law, 14, 39, 63, 73, 88, 96, 106, 117, 132
See also Turkish legal system/laws
Draft evasion (bakaya), 42, 51n31

E
Ebrahimian v. France, 123
Esen, Selin, 21, 22
Europe, 4, 13, 38–40, 47n2, 49n7, 74, 115
European Commission of Human Rights, 39, 119, 120
European Convention on Human Rights (ECHR), 2, 3, 8, 11, 12, 19, 29n1, 38, 39, 41, 45, 52n40, 52n41, 58, 60, 61, 63, 64, 70, 83, 85, 91, 93, 102, 107, 117, 132, 134n2
European Court of Human Rights (ECtHR), 3, 4, 8, 13–20, 22, 24–27, 29, 39–41, 49n12, 57, 58, 60–65, 69–72, 74, 84–92, 94, 98–103, 106, 117, 119–126, 129, 131–133
European Parliament, 39
European Union (EU)
 accession process, 5, 22, 41
 harmonization process, 4
 Progress Report, 70, 82, 91, 92, 106
Evren, Kenan, 67
Eweida and others v. United Kingdom, 131

F
Failure to attend the 'draft examination' (*yoklama kaçağı*), 42
Federation of Alevi Bektasi Associations, 17
Folgero and others v. Norway, 15, 60
Forum externum, 9–13, 38, 83, 92, 117
Forum internum, 2, 8–14, 18–20, 28, 38, 92, 117, 119

Freedom of thought, conscience and religion, 1, 2, 8–13, 19, 25, 28, 36–40, 46, 48n6, 50n15, 58, 70, 74, 83, 115–119, 125–127, 131, 132

G
Gamaleddyn v. France, 121
General Assembly, 118
General Comment, 10, 59, 83, 118
General Directorate of Foundations (*Vakıflar Genel Müdürlüğü*), 97, 102
Ghazal v. France, 121
Gönenç, Levent, 21, 22
Grand Chamber, 19, 39, 49n12, 103, 120, 122, 123
Greece, 14, 15, 87, 88, 93, 136n16
Greek, 14, 16, 21, 22, 82, 87, 89, 94, 95, 102, 104, 106, 107n1
Grzelak v. Poland, 61

H
Hamidović v. Bosnia and Herzegovina, 124
Hasan and Eylem Zengin v. Turkey, 4, 57, 61
Hassan and Chaouch v. Bulgaria, 89
Headscarf, 4, 115, 116, 120, 121, 123, 127–134
Human rights
 international law, 119
 violations, 2, 15, 17–20, 61, 63, 72, 87–90, 120
Human Rights Committee (HRC)
 concluding observations, 38
 General comment, 10, 59, 83, 118
 individual communications, 38

I

Ibero-American Convention on Young People's Rights, 36, 48n4
İçduygu, Ahmet, 22
İmam Hatip (vocational religious schools), 65, 67, 71
İmamoğlu, Ekrem, 101
Imprisonment, 36, 40, 42, 43
International Covenant on Civil and Political Rights (ICCPR), 2, 8–12, 29n1, 37, 38, 52n41, 58, 59, 83, 91, 117
International obligation, 22, 117
International standards, 74
İskenderun Military Hospital Medical Council, 46
Islam, 4, 8, 17–19, 21–24, 28, 62, 63, 67, 70, 71, 81, 82, 94, 97, 100, 105
Israel, 36, 43
İstanbul Metropolitan Municipality, 101
İzmir Metropolitan Municipality, 99, 101
İzzettin Doğan and others v. Turkey, 103

J

Jehovah's Witnesses, 4, 82, 87, 92, 98, 107n1
Jews, 22, 70, 106, 107n1
J. Singh v. France, 121
Justice and Development Party (*Adalet ve Kalkınma Partisi* – AKP), 2, 4, 101, 116

K

Karataş, Işıl, 133
Kavakçı, Merve, 129
Kenanoğlu, Ali, 101
Kervancı v. France, 121
Kestel Hacı Bektaş-ı Veli Culture Centre, 99
Koran, 62, 65, 71, 77–78n49
Kurtulmuş, Sevgi, 129

L

Lamiye Bulut v. Turkey, 120
Lautsi and others v. Italy, 122, 136n33
Law no. 657 on Public Servants, 128
Law on the Establishment and Jurisdiction of the Presidency of Religious Affairs, 69
Law on the Protection of Personal Data, 27
Legal personality, 4, 91, 92, 96, 101–103, 106
Leirvåg and ors v. Norway, 59

M

Manoussakis and others v. Greece, 87
Mansur Yalçın and others v. Turkey, 4, 57
Masaev v. Moldova, 88
Militarism, 41, 43–45
Military Courts Act, 42
Military-nation, 35–46
Military Penal Code, 42, 43, 54n58
Military service, 3, 19, 21, 35–40, 42–46, 48n4, 51n29
Military Service Act, 42
Military Supreme Court, 42
Minnesota Multiple Personality Inventory (MMPI), 45
Minority groups, 28, 93, 101
Murdoch, Jim, 11
Mutafyan, Mesrob, 104

N
National identity card, 7–29
Nationalist Action Party (*Milliyetçi Hareket Partisi*-MHP), 101
National Security Book, 45
National Security Council (*Milli Güvenlik Kurulu*-MGK), 44, 67
National service, 37, 42, 50n13
Non-believers, 3, 61
Non-derogable rights, 12
Non-governmental organisations, 2, 36
Non-Muslim(s), 4, 21, 22, 65, 68, 70, 82, 92, 94, 97, 98
North Atlantic Treaty Organization (NATO), 40

O
Odabaş, Dursun, 132
Open-mindedness, 1, 84
Organization for Security and Co-operation in Europe (OSCE), 129
Orthodox Church, 15, 87
Ottoman Empire, 4, 21, 65, 76n28, 93

P
Parliamentary Assembly of the Council of Europe (PACE), 39, 60
Partsch, Karl Josef, 9, 29n4
Paster, Amir, 43
Peker, Recep, 66
People's Republican Party (*Cumhuriyet Halk Partisi* – CHP), 101
Peoples' Democracy Party (*Halkların Demokratik Partisi* – HDP), 101
Places of worship, 4, 81–107

Pluralism, 1, 2, 19, 48n7, 63, 84, 89, 90
Population
  Population Register Law, 21
  Population Services Law, 21, 27
Prophet Muhammad, 71, 74
Protestant churches, 4, 98, 105
  Association of Protestant Churches, 99, 104

R
Recommendation 87/8 (PACE), 39
Recommendation 478 (PACE), 39
Recommendation 1720 (PACE), 60
Regulation Concerning the Dress of Personnel Employed in Public Institutions, 129, 138n71, 138n72
Religion, freedom of, 2, 3, 5, 8, 17, 20, 26, 73, 83, 85, 87, 90, 95, 100, 104, 106, 116, 118, 122, 128
Religious Culture and Ethics classes, 61, 62, 64, 72, 74, 77n49
Religious officials
  dede, 103
  religious leaders, 83, 96, 103–104
Religious symbols and dress, 4, 115–134
Republic of Turkey, *see* Turkey
Resolution 1989 (European Parliament), 39
Resolution 1994 (European Parliament), 39
Resolution 337 (PACE), 39
Resolution 2005/40 (Commission on Human Rights), 119
Right to teach one's religion and belief, 4
R. Singh v. France, 121

S

Şahin, Hatice Hasdemir, 131
Şahin, Leyla, 120, 131
Saktanber, Ayşe, 127
Saniewski v. Poland, 13, 60
Savda, Halil, 40, 43, 46
Sceptics, 1, 11
Secularism, 2, 3, 22–26, 28, 61, 66, 69, 95, 97, 116, 124, 125, 128–131, 133
Secular state, 2, 8, 22, 24, 61, 95, 128, 130–132
Şenay Karaduman v. Turkey, 120
Serif v. Greece, 19, 88
Shabbat, Itzik, 43
Sicil-i Nüfus Nizamnamesi, 21
Sinan Işık v Turkey, 26–27
Singh, Mann, 121
Sıtkı Baba Cemevi, 99
Sofianopoulos and others v. Greece, 14
Soyarık, Nalan, 22
Special Rapporteurs, 2
State Planning Organisation, 69
Stedman v. United Kingdom, 120
Sümela Monastery, 102
Sunni Islam, 4, 24, 28, 63, 81, 82, 97, 105
Syriac Chaldean, 94
Syrian Orthodox, 82

T

Tanyar and Küçükergin v. Turkey, 87
Tarhan, Mehmet, 40, 43, 53n57
Thought, freedom of, 1, 2, 8–13, 19, 25, 28, 36–40, 46, 48n6, 50n15, 58, 70, 74, 83, 115–119, 125–127, 131, 132
Tolerance, 1, 84, 126
Treaty of Lausanne, 4, 21, 70, 82, 93, 102, 106

Turkey, 2–5, 5n1, 7–9, 17, 20–28, 36, 38, 40–46, 47n3, 51n29, 52n41, 54n58, 57, 58, 61, 63–74, 76n28, 81, 82, 87, 88, 91–107, 107n1, 116, 117, 119, 120, 126–134, 136n16
See also Republic of Turkey
Turkish Army, 45, 46, 51n30
Turkish Civil Code, 102, 106, 127
Turkish courts, 3, 17, 52n40, 58, 82, 93
Turkish culture, 44
Turkish legal system/laws, 41
Turkish Ministry of Justice, 64
Turkish Ministry of National Education, 64, 65
Turkish nation, 44
Turkish National Assembly, 63
Turkish parliament, 22, 66, 129
Turkishness, 8, 46, 105
Turkish Penal Code, 42, 43, 127

U

Ülke, Osman Murat, 40
Ülke v. Turkey, 40
Unfit report(s), 45–46
Union of Soviet Socialist Republics (USSR), 136n16
United Kingdom (UK), 136n16
United Nations (UN), 2, 9, 36–38, 40, 46, 49n8, 58, 82, 118, 119
Special Rapporteur on Freedom of Religion or Belief, 2, 5n1
United States of America (USA), 40, 65, 104, 136n16
United States Commission on International Religious Freedom, 2, 94

Universal Declaration of Human
   Rights (UDHR), 2, 8, 29n1,
   36, 58, 117
Üsküdar Municipality, 105

V
Venice Commission, 91–94, 97
Virtue Party (*Fazilet Partisi*), 129

W
Welfare Party (*Refah Partisi*), 128
Women, 4, 45, 51n30, 127, 128, 130

Women's Rights
   Organisation Against
   Discrimination, 128

Y
Yalman, Aytaç, 46
Yezidis, 82
Yorulmaz, Uğur, 41
Yücel, Hasan Ali, 66

Z
Zoroastrian, 27

CPSIA information can be obtained
at www.ICGtesting.com
Printed in the USA
LVHW081927020421
683323LV00003B/278